"*Tom Paine for the 21st century. A surprisingly compelling argument for applying the small-is-beautiful philosophy to the United States itself.*"

—Jay Walljasper
Editor of *Ode* magazine

"*I must assure you of my pleasure in, and approval of, your views on the **Second Vermont Republic**. The assertion by Vermonters of a sensible foreign policy is wonderfully to the good. You have my agreement and my admiration.*"

—John Kenneth Galbraith
Harvard Economist

"*All power to Vermont in its effort to distinguish itself from the U.S.A. as a whole, and to pursue in its own way the cultivation of its tradition. My enthusiasm for what you are trying to do in Vermont remains undiminished; I am happy for any small support I can give it.*"

—George F. Kennan
Former Ambassador to Russia and
Professor, Institute for Advanced Studies, Princeton

SECESSION

SECESSION

HOW VERMONT AND ALL THE OTHER STATES CAN SAVE THEMSELVES FROM THE EMPIRE

BY THOMAS H. NAYLOR

FOREWORD BY KIRKPATRICK SALE

Feral House

ISBN: 978-1-932595-30-7

Feral House
1240 W. Sims Way #124
Port Townsend, WA 98368

www.FeralHouse.com

10 9 8 7 6 5 4 3 2 1

For further information about the Secession movement, see:
www.vermontrepublic.org
middleburyinstitute.org

This book was printed on recycled paper.

Design by Bill Smith

CONTENTS

DEDICATION

This manifesto was inspired by former Ambassador George F. Kennan, dean of the American diplomatic corps, American patriot, and Vermont aficionado, to whom it is dedicated.

For over seventy-five years, Ambassador Kennan was at the cutting edge of American foreign policy. When he died on 17 March 2005, at the age of 101, few Americans were aware that he supported the peaceful break-up of the American Empire and the creation of a Vermont independence movement.

Although best known as the father of "containment," the mainstay of American Cold War foreign policy, Kennan first revealed his radical decentralist tendencies in his 1993 book *Around the Cragged Hill*. "We are… a monster country… And there is a real question as to whether 'bigness' in a body politic is not an evil in itself, quite aside from the policies pursued in its name." He also noted "a certain lack of modesty in the national self-image" of the U.S. He proposed decentralizing the U.S. into a "dozen constituent republics" including New England, the Middle Atlantic states, the Middle West, the Northwest, the Southwest (including Hawaii), Texas, the Old South, Florida, Alaska, New York City, Chicago, and Los Angeles. "To these entities I would accord a larger part of the present federal powers than one might suspect—large enough, in fact, to make most people gasp."

After reading Kennan's final book, *An American Family* (2000), which describes the life of his family in Waterbury, Vermont in the late eighteenth and early nineteenth centuries, I wrote to him in January 2001 and sent him a copy of my book with William H. Willimon entitled *Downsizing the U.S.A. (1997),* a book which unabashedly called for Vermont independence as a first step towards the peaceful dissolution of the Union. His letter of 7 February 2001 was the first of ten letters and several phone calls which I received from him over the next two years. In it he noted "the closeness of many of our views" and added, "we are, I fear, a lonely band…"

In a letter dictated to his secretary Terrie Bramley on 22 October 2001 Kennan responded to my proposal that Vermont join Maine, New Hampshire, and the Atlantic provinces of Canada to create a country the size of Denmark. In this letter he said, "I see nothing fanciful and nothing towards the realization of which efforts of enlightened people might not be usefully directed." He concluded by writing, "I thought you, more than anyone else of my acquaintance, ought to know the directions in which my thoughts are leading in this late stage in my own life."

On 1 May 2002 he wrote, "All power to Vermont in its effort to distinguish itself from the U.S.A. as a whole, and to pursue in its own way the cultivation of its own tradition." His most poignant letter, handwritten on 1 August 2002, said, "My enthusiasm for what you are trying to do in Vermont remains undiminished, and I am happy for any small support I can give it."

In his last letter to me on 14 February 2003, two days before his 99th birthday and just prior to the war in Iraq, he expressed concern about the negative political impact that the war might have on the Vermont independence movement. On this he was mistaken. The war that began on March 19 of that year actually gave impetus to the movement which had been officially launched two weeks earlier and soon became known as the Second Vermont Republic.

Although I never heard from him again, George Kennan was a major source of inspiration for the Second Vermont Republic. He provided valuable insights about the size of America, the degree to which it is centralized, and its tendency towards imperialism. He also appreciated Vermont's uniqueness—its history, its culture, and its size. Above all, he gave me the courage to pursue my dream of an independent Vermont. Unknown to him, he was truly the godfather of the Second Vermont Republic movement. It is my fervent wish that he may someday be known as the godfather of The Second Vermont Republic itself.

FOREWORD

There have been a number of books about secession in recent years, but none as powerful and useful as this one, because it not only lays out a convincing case for secession from the American Empire but provides a working model of how an American state might really go about achieving that. Thomas Naylor, the founder and chair of the Second Vermont Republic, perhaps now the foremost active secessionist organization in the country, has here charted a brave and inspiring course for any American interested in practical, useful, thoroughgoing social and political change in America.

Secession may seem like an outlandish idea at first, but when considered forthrightly and unprejudicially it becomes a powerful alternative to other kinds of political action—as a group of people discovered at a meeting called a Radical Consultation in Middlebury, Vermont, in November 2004. Let me tell you how it went.

For a whole day we thought through the possible strategies open to a serious American interested in working for a fundamental alteration of the national government we suffer under and creating societies responsive to basic human needs.

We began with elective politics, the idea of voting for the same old Democrats and Republicans, but it didn't take long to reject that as futile: *they* were the ones we wanted to change, after all, they had proved time and again how beholden they were to the corporate masters who pay for their campaigns, and votes. And we took no time in rejecting the reformist lobby-Congress trap that so many environmental and liberal-cause groups spend so much money and effort on, since that was, after all, trying to change those same elected officials.

Next we considered the third-party alternative, thinking of Perot's and Nader's influence on national politics, and concluded that they did so poorly, despite considerable money and media attention, because the two major parties had essentially rigged the system so that outsiders couldn't win. Besides, launching a party and fighting an election on a national scale involves getting money and support from the same kinds of people and organizations that contribute to the other parties, and in the process becoming beholden to them.

So if reformism in all its guises is rejected, what other means of action are there for serious change? There's always revolt and revolution, of course, but it didn't take much deliberation to decide that there was no way, even if there were trained militia bands and some weaponry smuggled in by separatist sympathizers in Canada, a serious revolution could be mounted in this country today. And no reason to doubt that Washington would use its most potent weaponry to crush it if it arose.

And that leaves secession—instead of reforming or attacking the corrupt and corporatist system, leave it. At first glance, it seemed like a crazy idea to many, and maybe as dangerous as a revolution—after all, the last time anybody in this country tried secession, they were ruthlessly attacked and eventually destroyed. But the more we considered it, it seemed like a reasonable option, particularly if it was done peaceably and openly.

It is in the grand American tradition—the war of the colonies against the British Empire was not a war of revolution, for no one wanted to take over London, but of secession, leaving the empire; and there was even a peaceable tradition, for Maine seceded from Massachusetts peaceably, Tennessee from North Carolina, and Kentucky and West Virginia from Virginia. It could justifiably be seen as legal and constitutional, since three of the colonies wrote provisions allowing them to secede before joining the Union, there is nothing in the Constitution forbidding it, and the fact that Congress considered passing a law against it in 1861 but failed to do so indicates it was not then considered unlawful.

It could be done practically and democratically, either by a vote among all citizens of voting age with, say, a two-thirds majority, or by a two-third (or other large) vote of the legislature of a state. Upon such a vote and a declaration of independence delivered to Washington, a seceding state could immediately appeal to the world, apply to the United Nations, and seek diplomatic support particularly from the fifteen republics that seceded from the Soviet Union and the seven nations that seceded from Yugoslavia, and Norway (which seceded from Sweden, Belgium (from France), plus all the colonies that declared independence from European empires.

And its especial appeal would be that not only does it allow a state (or region) to remove itself from the taxes, regulations, entangling alliances, bloated bureaucracy, and corrupting forms of governance of the national government, it allows a state to regain some measure of democracy, some hands-on control over the decisions that effect its life.

We ended the Radical Consultation with a strong feeling that secession was a very powerful tool for promoting self-determination, democracy and independence, but also a powerful idea that could spread widely throughout this continent, as it has spread widely throughout the world since 1945. (The U.N. began with 50 nations—it now has 195.) And if it took hold in even a half-dozen likely places (Alaska, Hawaii, Puerto Rico, Texas, the South, Vermont New Hampshire), it would rapidly create a great change in the American Empire and the way it works, probably leading to its eventual demise.

The final act of the conference was to issue a Middlebury Declaration, the full text of which is quoted later on in this book. The final part reads:

> *"There is no reason that we cannot begin to examine the processes of secession in the United States. There are already at least 28 separatist organizations in this country and there seems to be a growing sentiment that, because the national government has shown itself to be clumsy, unresponsive, and unaccountable in so many ways, power should be concentrated at lower levels. Whether these levels should be the states or coherent regions within the states or something smaller still is a matter best left to the people active in devolution, but the principle of secession must be established as valid and legitimate.*
>
> *"To this end, therefore, we are pledged to create a movement that will place secession on the national agenda, encourage nonviolent secessionist organizations throughout the country, develop communication among existing and future secessionist groups, and create a body of scholarship to examine and promote the ideas and principles of secessionism."*

And so it seemed only logical that we establish a think-tank to promote these ends, and that was done in a few months following the meeting. It is called the Middlebury Institute, in honor of that initial conference, and though it is not in fact located in that city, it embodies the principles and hopes and politics that were engendered there.

This book is an important part of that process of creating a movement. It is a beacon not only for the good citizens of Vermont but for all those wishing to dismantle the American Empire and create real independent democracies in its stead.

Kirkpatrick Sale
Director, Middlebury Institute

A EULOGY FOR THE
FIRST VERMONT REPUBLIC

4 MARCH 1791

Ladies and gentlemen, it is my solemn duty to inform you that on 4 March 1791 the First Vermont Republic, the only American republic which truly invented itself, entered immortality and became the fourteenth state of the American Empire. Fourteen years after declaring its independence, Vermont was seduced into the Union by the promise of Life, Liberty, and the Pursuit of Happiness. Over two hundred years later the Green Mountain state finds itself in a nation whose government condones the annihilation of Afghanistan and Iraq, a war on terrorism which it helped create, the illegal rendition of terrorist suspects, prisoner abuse and torture, citizen surveillance, the Military Commissions Act, corporate greed, pandering to the rich and powerful, a culture of deceit, and a foreign policy based on full spectrum dominance, imperial overstretch, and unconditional support for Israel.

A state convention convened by the Vermont Assembly on 10 January 1791 petitioned the United States Congress for admission into the Union. By a vote of 105 to 4 the delegates of the convention opted to sell the soul of the independent Republic of Vermont to the Empire. Vermont's statehood petition was ratified by the U.S. Congress on 4 March, a day that will go down in history as a day of infamy.

America was supposed to have been immortal, but in the end it could not deliver. Its government has lost its moral authority. It has no soul. As a nation it has become unsustainable and unfixable because it is effectively ungovernable. The endgame is near.

Is it possible that out of the ashes of the First Vermont Republic a Second Vermont Republic might emerge? Might not Vermont experience a kind of resurrection from the dead, or at least from its two-century long slumber, resulting in a new state of consciousness opposed to the tyranny of corporate America and the U.S. government and committed to once again becoming an independent republic? Might such a republic embrace these principles: political independence, human scale, sustainability, economic solidarity, power sharing, equal opportunity, tension reduction, and mutuality?

What if tiny Vermont, the second smallest state in the Union, were to become an example for other states to follow leading to the peaceful dissolution of the largest, most powerful empire of all time—the United States of America? Literally every reason why Vermont might want to opt out of the Union is equally applicable to every other state. Vermont's paradigm for secession could easily be adapted to any other state.

Is it possible that the Green Mountain state might actually help save America from itself and help save the rest of the world from America by seceding from the Union and leading the nation into peaceful disunion?

In the words of Reverend Ben T. Matchstick, we pray for Vermont independence "in the name of the flounder, the sunfish, and the holy mackerel."

Amen

THE MANIFESTO

Thoughtful Vermonters, opposed to the tyranny of the United States government, Corporate America, and globalization, believe that Vermont should once again become an independent republic as it was between 1777 and 1791, and that the United States of America should begin to peacefully dissolve.

FIRST, we find it increasingly difficult to protect ourselves from the debilitating effects of big government, big business, big markets, and big agriculture, who want all of us to be the same and to love bigness as much as they do.

SECOND, in addition to being too big, our government is too centralized, too powerful, too intrusive, too materialistic, and too unresponsive to the needs of individual citizens and small communities. Massive military spending, huge budget deficits, and a mounting trade deficit are all part of the problem.

THIRD, the U.S. government has lost its moral authority because it is owned, operated, and controlled by corporate America. National and Congressional elections are bought and sold to the highest bidders.

FOURTH, we have a single political party, the Republican Party, disguised as a two-party system. The comatose Democratic Party is effectively brain dead, having had no new ideas since the 1960s.

FIFTH, we have become disillusioned with the so-called American way—corporate greed, an addiction to fossil fuels, the war on terrorism, citizen surveillance, rendition of terrorist suspects, prisoner abuse and torture, the suppression of civil liberties, pandering to the rich and powerful, pseudo-religious drivel, environmental insensitivity, and the culture of deceit.

SIXTH, American foreign policy, which is based on the doctrine of full spectrum dominance, is immoral, illegal, unconstitutional, and in violation of the United Nations Charter.

SEVENTH, as long as Vermont remains in the Union, we face the risk of terrorist attack and military conscription of our youth.

EIGHTH, the U.S. suffers from imperial overstretch and has become unsustainable politically, economically, agriculturally, socially, culturally, and environmentally. It has become both ungovernable and unfixable.

"Whenever any form of government becomes destructive... it is the right of the people to alter or to abolish it, and to institute new government, laying its foundation on such principles and organizing its powers in such form, as to them shall seem most likely to effect their safety and happiness," said Thomas Jefferson in the Declaration of Independence. Just as a group has a right to form, so too does it have a right to disband, to subdivide itself, or to withdraw from a larger unit.

Vermont is smaller, more rural, more democratic, less violent, less commercial, more egalitarian, more humane, more independent, and more radical than most states. It provides a communitarian alternative to the dehumanized, mass-production, mass-consumption, narcissistic lifestyle which pervades most of America.

Fundamental to what it means to be a Vermonter is the right of self-preservation. The time has come for us peacefully to rebel against the American empire by (1) regaining control of our lives from big government, big business, big cities, big schools, and big computer networks; (2) relearning how to take care of ourselves by decentralizing, downsizing, localizing, demilitarizing, simplifying, and humanizing our lives; and (3) learning how to help others take care of themselves.

This is a call for Vermont to reclaim its soul—to return to its rightful status as an independent republic. In so doing, Vermont can provide a kinder, gentler model for a nation obsessed with money, power, size, speed, greed, and fear of terrorism.

Long live the Second Vermont Republic! If you live in Vermont, come join us. If you live outside Vermont, please support us, and please consider the possibility of starting your own independence movement as well.

Chapter 1

THE ENDGAME FOR AMERICA

A unipolar world has one single center of power, one single center of force, one single center of decision-making, one master, and one sovereign. At the end of the day this is pernicious not only for all those within this system, but also for the sovereign itself because it destroys itself from within. It lacks the moral foundations of modern civilization.

{ Vladimir V. Putin, 10 February, 2007 }

Who could have imagined back in 1982, when stultified Leonid I. Brezhnev was still in charge of the Soviet geriocracy and the Cold War was still raging, that within seven years the six Eastern European allies of the Soviet Union would be set free and that two years later the Evil Empire would cease to exist? And who could possibly have imagined that this would all be achieved nonviolently (with the exception of Romania), by undermining the credibility and legitimacy of the respective communist regimes?

Not unlike other great empires, the Soviet Empire was simply unsustainable economically, politically, and militarily. It had become an economic and social basket case as well as an environmental disaster. It was fundamentally unmanageable. It was too big, too intrusive, too materialistic, too militarized, too imperialistic, too violent, too undemocratic, and too unresponsive to the needs of individual citizens and local communities. In addition, it contained too many heterogeneous republics, ethnic minorities, religions, and nationalities to be run by a handful of self-appointed bureaucrats in Moscow. The time had come for the Soviet Empire to die. It had lost its moral authority. It had no soul.

But why was all of this so surprising to American Sovietologists and the United States government? Why did so few "experts" on the Soviet Union anticipate the rapidity of its precipitous decline? Until the empire crumbled, American foreign policy was predicated on the assumption that it was business as usual in the Soviet Union.

A cursory study of world history reveals a self-evident truth. No major empire anywhere at any time in history has ever proven to be *sustainable*. Sustainability refers to the ability of a community, a town, a city, or a nation-state to ensure the availability of political, economic, agricultural, social, cultural, and environmental resources for future generations. The British, Chinese, Egyptians, French, Germans, Greeks, Japanese, Romans, Turks, and Soviets have all presided over megaempires, some spanning entire continents as well as centuries. None survived the test of time. In the end, many of them crumbled in rapid and unexpected ways like the Soviet Union. They all inevitably fail, according to Kirkpatrick Sale, "because of their size, complexity, territorial reach, stratification, heterogeneity, domination, hierarchy, and inequalities."

And what about the United States, the most powerful nation in history economically and militarily, the world's first truly global superpower? Is there any reason to believe it will prove to be an exception to the rule?

Our government's dogged, mean-spirited, often illegal, zero-sum pursuit of the war on terrorism, along with a foreign policy based on full spectrum dominance and imperial overstretch, appears to be leading us into our own death spiral. So too is the unwavering commitment to globalization at any cost, including environmental degradation. There is resounding evidence that it is only a matter of time before corporate behemoths implode, and then the fragile house-of-cards economy along with its rarefied stock market collapses. Not only has our highly polarized nation become virtually ungovernable, but it has most probably become unsustainable politically, militarily, economically, agriculturally, socially, culturally, and environmentally.

POLITICS

Like the former Soviet Union, we have a single-party political system in the United States, though here it is masked as a two-party system. The Democratic Party is effectively brain dead and has not had an original idea since the 1960s. On all matters related to foreign policy it marches in lock step with the Republicans. Both parties are firmly entrenched in the centralist camp—committed to making us all the same and all dependent on a central national government. In spite of the differences in their rhetoric and styles, they both want life in the United States to be bigger, faster, more complex, more commercial, more high-tech, more energy-dependent, more globally interdependent, more militaristic, and more regulated. They both provide unconditional support for the apartheid state of Israel. Neither party has a peaceful geopolitical strategy for confronting the problems of peak oil or global warming.

Billions of dollars are spent on national and state elections. Our government is a cross between an oligarchy and an autocracy disguised as a democracy. So turned off are most Americans by the influence of campaign contributions and the absence of choice in our political system that most of us do not even bother to vote.

IMPERIALISM

Imperialism refers to the practice of forming and maintaining an empire through military, political, or economic conquest. Like every other large empire, the history of the United States is firmly grounded on imperialism—both external imperialism and internal imperialism.

Although our nation was founded on the principles of life, liberty, and the pursuit of happiness, the story of how Native Americans were relentlessly forced to abandon their homes and lands and move into Indian territories to make room for American states is a story of arrogance, greed, and raw military power. Our barbaric conquest of the Native Americans continued for several hundred years and involved many of our most cherished national heroes, including George Washington, Thomas Jefferson, James Monroe, and Andrew Jackson. We have violated over three hundred treaties which we signed protecting the rights of American Indians.

Not only was the United States the last major country to abolish slavery, but we were the only country to do so violently. Not surprisingly, many of our founding fathers who fought the Indians were also slave owners.

The American military defeats of England, Mexico, and Spain in the nineteenth century and the annexations of Texas, Oregon, New Mexico, and California were rationalized on the basis of "Manifest Destiny" or "God's will." So too were our interventions in Cuba, Puerto Rico, Hawaii, and the Philippines.

Although lauded by most for freeing the slaves, Abraham Lincoln can also be seen as the father of American internal imperialism, as Thomas J. DiLorenzo points out in his book *The Real Lincoln*. Lincoln invaded the Confederate States without the consent of Congress, suspended habeas corpus, imprisoned thousands of American citizens without a trial for opposing his policies, censored all telegraph communications, imprisoned dozens of opposition newspaper publishers, nationalized the railroads, used Federal troops to interfere with elections, confiscated firearms, and deported an opposition member of Congress—always in the name of freedom and democracy.

World War I, the Great Depression, World War II, and the Cold War resulted in countless acts of internal imperialism against individuals as well as state and local governments. Heavy-handed New Deal programs, the detention of Japanese Americans in California, the military draft, McCarthyism, "urban renewal" programs, and the indiscriminate arrest and inhumane treatment of Arab men as part of the war on terrorism are but a few examples of domestic imperialism.

Conservative economist Llewelyn H. Rockwell, Jr. has succinctly summarized the record of domestic imperialism of the first four years of Team Bush.

> *Bush nationalized airport security, created the largest bureaucracy in history in the form of Homeland Security, tossed our constitutional protections we used to take for granted, enacted the largest expansion of welfare in three generations with the prescription drug benefit, intruded into local schools as never before with No Child Left Behind, brought many industries under protectionist regulation, and undertook two major wars that have cost hundreds of billions and left only destruction and chaos in their wake. Clinton increased spending 13.4 percent in his first term and 16 percent in his second, but Bush's first-term spending soared +29.*
>
> *Any attempt by the federal government to democratize the whole rather than its parts can lead to internal imperialism. This is particularly true of federal social programs such as affirmative action, occupational safety, handicapped education, Medicare, Medicaid, family assistance, and minimum wage laws. The so-called No Child Left Behind law is a not-so-subtle attempt to McDonaldize our public schools.*

When one contemplates the American political system, the words that come to mind are apathy, inertia, and atrophy, not sustainability—just like back in the U.S.S.R.

In the words of Kirkpatrick Sale, "Empires, because they are by definition colonizers, are always forced to extend their military reach farther and farther, and enlarge it against unwilling colonies more and more, until coffers are exhausted, communication lines are overextended, troops are unreliable, and the periphery resists and ultimately revolts."

The terrorist attacks on New York City and Washington have cast doubt on the sustainability of an American foreign policy that is based on two fundamental premises. First, political, economic, technological, and military might make right. Second, the rest of the world should be just like us. To enforce this policy the U.S. maintains a military presence in 153 countries. It has intervened in the affairs of 22 countries since the end of World War II, and none of these interventions was preceded by a declaration of war. The most recent victims have been Grenada, Libya, Panama, Iraq, Somalia, Haiti, Sudan, Serbia, and Afghanistan. America loves to play the role of the global bully—particularly since presidential popularity ratings always soar after we attack some powerless nation. Since 2001 our government has turned up its nose at all forms of multilateralism, with the exception of the American-dictated war on terrorism. It unilaterally abandoned a global warming treaty, rejected protocols enforcing a ban on germ warfare, demanded amendments to an accord on illegal sales of small arms, threatened to boycott an internal conference on racism, and walked away from the 1972 Antiballistic Missile Treaty with the former Soviet Union—the bedrock on which all subsequent arms control treaties with Russia rest.

Surely they must have been kidding, if we were supposed to have believed that on 11 September 2001, nineteen Muslim fanatics armed only with boxcutters pulled off the greatest act of terrorism in history under the command of a charismatic, sinister-looking, wealthy, CIA-trained, Muslim fundamentalist, Saudi named Osama bin Laden from his high-tech cave in the rugged mountains of Afghanistan. Without one shred of evidence, our government claims that these Arab terrorists commandeered four jetliners, brought down the Twin Towers of the World Trade Center, severely damaged the Pentagon, and almost succeeded in destroying the White House and the Capitol. And they did all of this because they "hated freedom"

Anyone questioning the details of this incredible tale is said to be a "conspiracy theorist" and is not to be taken seriously. And what about the anthrax scare which followed on the heels of 9/11 and no longer even shows up on the national radar screen?

If 9/11 were the work of Muslim terrorists, how is it possible that six years later not a single Muslim suicide bomber had managed to surface anywhere in the United States? If Islamofascism is the threat we are told it is by our government, surely a random suicide bomber would have found his way into the Super Bowl, Madison Square Garden, or Times Square on New Year's Eve and killed a few hundred people. But there has been no such event. Absolutely nothing!

11 September 2001 may very well be remembered as the beginning of the end of the American Empire as we know it today. Amidst a sea of American flags and patriotic fervor, our militaristic government called for national unity, revenge against Afghanistan, increased government surveillance, the curtailment of civil liberties, beefed-up domestic antiterrorist activity, an international coalition to seek out and destroy terrorists worldwide, and an end to states such as Iran, Iraq, and North Korea which were alleged to sponsor terrorism. Every time our president opened his mouth, the price of gold went up and the United States became a little less sustainable. Gold is well known to be a safe haven investment of last resort. When the world is going to hell in a hand basket, people invest in gold.

After 9/11, Osama bin Laden soon became the new Che Guevara of the poor, the powerless, and the disenfranchised worldwide. For every Muslim fundamentalist killed in Afghanistan, Iran, Iraq, Pakistan, or elsewhere—or arrested by the FBI in the United States, Germany, or England—another hundred Arab, African, Asian, or Latin American dissidents were radicalized.

Our one-sided support of Israel, our stubborn refusal to end the embargo with Iraq, our cozy relationship with Saudi Arabia and other undemocratic Arab oil-producing states, our attempt to annihilate tiny, impoverished Afghanistan, and the involuntary "regime change" and occupation of Iraq have paved the way for World War III—a never-ending war with Islam combined with a global war between the haves and have-nots. There appears to be no interest whatsoever in sorting out the real reasons underlying Muslim rage against America.

Revenge was the only game in town—revenge against Afghanistan, where bin Laden was thought to be hiding; and revenge against alleged Al Qaeda ally Iraq, where Saddam Hussein was said to have weapons of mass destruction. Both countries were annihilated, Hussein captured, and later executed. No weapons of mass destruction were found and no Iraq/Al Qaeda connection ever corroborated. U.S. occupation of Iraq proved to be an unmitigated disaster, and terrorism has continued unabated in Madrid, London, Egypt, India, Indonesia, Jordan, and throughout the world.

With its unprovoked, illegal, unilateral, pre-emptive "shock and awe" conquest of Iraq and its treatment of prisoners at Abu Ghraib and elsewhere, the United States sacrificed its credibility and moral authority. In so doing, we also managed to alienate most of our closest allies (except Britain), millions of Muslims, and much of the rest of the world. We are no longer a nation governed by the rule of law but rather by the law of the jungle. Anything goes! Whatever the Empire wants, the Empire gets. Who will be next? Iran, Syria, Palestine, Cuba, Venezuela, Nigeria, or us?

Is it possible that the real purpose of the so-called war on terror is to demonize Islam among Americans and Europeans so as to justify hegemonizing the supply of oil in the Middle East to keep our economic engine running?

So large is the U.S. military budget that it will soon exceed the combined military spending of all of the countries in the rest of the world. It's just a matter of time before the Pentagon reinstates compulsory military service, a particularly onerous form of internal imperialism. How many Americans are prepared to die or sacrifice their children to make the world safe for McDonald's, Wal-Marts, Fox News, gas-guzzling Hummers, Google, Bill Gates, and the rest of the Forbes 400 richest Americans?

With its policy of full spectrum dominance, the United States runs the risk of what Yale historian Paul Kennedy calls imperial overstretch, in which the sum of our nation's global commitments to Europe, Korea, Japan, and the Middle East exceeds its power to defend them and itself from rogue states or anyone else. Just as the Roman, Napoleonic, British, and Soviet empires were brought down by a leaching away from within rather than by an external threat, so too could the American Empire be brought down. If the Empire implodes, how much of the rest of the world will it take with it?

Economics

The vaunted communist propaganda of the Soviet Union was not half as effective as our government, our media, and our academic experts have been in promulgating the lies, myths, and half-truths perpetrated by Wall Street, corporate America, and Silicon Valley about the benefits of globalization and the Internet. Before the e-bubble burst and the prices of high-tech stocks came crashing back to earth, millions had turned to cyberspace for everything from information, employment, business, shopping, entertainment, and low-cost telecommunications to more transcendental benefits such as spirituality, worship, meaning, and community. Bill Clinton called the Net "our new town square." College graduates saw the Internet as a ticket to fame, fortune, financial security, self-actualization, and grassroots democracy. The Net was their virtual God.

The intense frenzy with which the ubiquitous Internet was embraced was reminiscent of the nineteenth-century California gold rush. Americans were mesmerized by the techno-hype and cant dished out by Silicon Valley. Former Federal Reserve Chairman Alan Greenspan described the Clinton boom at various times as a "once-in-a-generation frenzy of speculation" driven by "irrational exuberance" and "infectious greed."

Pundits claimed that e-business, the use of PCs and the Internet within a firm, would radically transform the way megacompanies do business by extending without limit their ability to reduce average costs as output increases. However, the number of megamergers which have gone sour casts doubt on such thinking.

The collapse of the giant energy trading company Enron and telecommunications megacompany WorldCom provided at least a temporary wake-up call for Wall Street, corporate America, the accounting profession, and the U.S. government. One of the greatest financial scandals of all time, Enron was a deceptive mixture of off-shore business, off-the-books loans, fake data, and creative accounting covered up by the firm's auditor Arthur Andersen. The $107 billion collapse of WorldCom resulted in the largest bankruptcy filing in American history. Unfortunately, Enron and WorldCom proved to be the tip of the iceberg as one major company after another was accused of shady bookkeeping or other misdeeds. Apparently, creative accounting has become the rule among all too many Fortune 500 companies.

When the Securities and Exchange Commission, state prosecutors, and market regulators announced a settlement with a dozen of the biggest Wall Street firms for conflicts of interest by their stock analysts, it amounted to little more than a slap on the wrist. These same firms pressed Congress to prevent the states from pursing further charges against those, such as themselves, who violate security laws.

Claims that information technology, the communication revolution, deregulation, and globalization will so alter the Goldilocks economy that increased productivity, record-high profits, levitating stock market prices, strong economic growth and job creation, low unemployment, and scant inflation will surely last forever have yet to be tested. Take airlines, for example. Five American airlines have already filed for bankruptcy. Others are likely to follow suit, as jet fuel prices continue to rise.

The Internet enables large companies to respond instantaneously to signs of softness in the economy and consumer demand by announcing plant closings and layoffs of tens of thousands. But when dozens of companies can do exactly the same thing, we soon can have recessions created at the speed of thought.

A cover-page in *Business Week* 3 February 2003 entitled "Is Your Job Next?" reported that, "a new round of globalization is sending upscale jobs offshore." The Big Three American automakers have announced plans to close dozens of automobile plants, laying off tens of thousands of high-paid employees. With millions of real manufacturing jobs exported offshore, who is going to be able to afford to buy all of the stuff required to keep the American economic engine running? Jobs lost abroad, through outsourcing and otherwise, are gone forever, and the impact of these job losses will eventually affect consumer spending.

Our staggering federal debt, trade deficit, and consumer debt could trigger a run on the dollar leading to inflation and high interest rates. Given our appetite for imported oil and foreign-made plastic yuck, a falling dollar would precipitate higher prices for imported goods. It would also make U.S. Treasury bonds less attractive to foreign investors, thus necessitating higher long-term interest rates to induce them to continue holding our government's debt.

The deeper we sink into the political and military quagmire in Iraq, the more likely we are to experience even larger government deficits, higher interest rates, increased inflation, and a collapse of the dollar. All of these problems will be further confounded if we invade Iran.

If foreign creditors ever become spooked by the size of the federal debt and our huge current-account deficit, confidence in the dollar could plunge, resulting in the sale of billions of dollars worth of treasury bills and bonds and thus sparking a global monetary crisis. In turn, the Federal Reserve Bank would be compelled to raise interest rates sharply to attract foreign credit. A major recession would follow.

Not unlike corporate America, our government employs smoke-and-mirrors accounting practices to deflect public opinion away from the magnitude of our staggering federal deficit. The cost of the war in Iraq and the cost of refinancing Social Security are conveniently left out of the U.S. budget. What is truly amazing is that Wall Street pretends not to notice this oversight.

Conservative Republican author Kevin Phillips has noted that the gap between the rich and the poor in the United States is greater than that of any other industrial democracy. "The imbalance of wealth and democracy in the United States is unsustainable," he argues.

Nothing better illustrates Phillips's point than the compensation of senior executives of major American companies. During the 1990s the average CEO's paycheck increased by a factor of six. According to *Business Week*, average total compensation (including salary, bonus, retirement benefits, incentive plan, and stock option gains) for the CEOs of the 365 largest American companies is now 500 times the average wage of a blue-collar worker. Until recently, Japanese and German CEOs were earning only 20 times what average factory workers earn. The retirement package of former Exxon Mobil CEO Lee R. Raymond amounted to nearly $400 million.

According to Princeton economist Paul Krugman, "The 13,000 richest families in America now have almost as much income as the 20 million poorest. And those 13,000 families have incomes 300 times that of average families." The combined net worth of the *Forbes* 400 richest people in America reached $1.25 trillion in 2006. All 400 were billionaires, and the top ten each had net worths of $15 billion or more. Heading this list was Bill Gates, whose net worth topped out at $90 billion before a federal judge charged Microsoft with violating the Sherman Antitrust Act. At that time the net worth of the poorest 40 percent of the American population was less than that of the Microsoft czar all by himself.

We live in a McDonaldized, high-tech, Wal-Mart economy in which little is manufactured here, nearly everything is imported from China, and we pay for it along with expensive foreign oil by manipulating the stock market and the real estate market and borrowing money from the Chinese. To keep wages as low as possible many employers no longer provide health insurance, pensions, or other fringe benefits. We call this unsustainable race to the bottom "progress."

Any combination of the following events could easily precipitate a major economic meltdown in the United States: (1) the end of the availability of cheap oil, (2) a continuation of the hemorrhaging of real jobs lost through globalization, (3) spiraling federal deficits driven by open-ended military budgets, (4) an ever-increasing trade deficit, (5) a precipitous decline in the value of the dollar, (6) a collapse of the real estate bubble, (7) a complete loss of confidence in financial information provided by Wall Street, and (8) a further widening of the income and wealth gap between the rich and the poor. Such an economic meltdown could well lead to social and even political upheavals.

AGRICULTURE

Yet another form of unsustainability in America is the demise of the family farm. High energy costs, the increased cost of mechanization, depressed farm prices, a government farm subsidy program that primarily benefits huge corporate farms, and the purchasing policies of the fast-food industry have all taken their toll on small family farms.

In the book *Fast Food Nation*, Eric Schlosser makes a convincing case that the fast-food industry has played a major role in transforming the American beef, pork, chicken, and potato industries into a handful of megacorporations that have almost total market control over the small farmers and producers who supply them. McDonald's is the nation's largest buyer of beef, pork, and potatoes, and the second largest buyer of chicken behind KFC (Kentucky Fried Chicken).

According to Schlosser, the top four meatpacking firms—ConAgra, IBP, Excel, and National Beef—slaughter 84 percent of the nation's cattle, and eight chicken processors control two-thirds of the American market. Schlosser claims that meatpacking is the most dangerous job in the United States, with working conditions in the vehemently anti-union industry among the worst anywhere in the world. He further points out that a single fast-food hamburger now contains meat from dozens or even hundreds of different cattle. The effects of tainted beef could literally reverberate around the world.

How many people feel comfortable eating genetically altered, taste-free fruits and vegetables grown and saturated with herbicides and pesticides on California megafarms and allowed to ripen during shipment across the continent? Yet small farmers—particularly organic farmers—who might provide alternatives cannot compete with the economic advantages of pesticides, chemical fertilizers, growth hormones, and genetically altered crops and farm animals.

Large corporate farms and the few giant buyers of agricultural products such as McDonald's, KFC, ConAgra, and IBP are to small family farms what monopolists such as Wal-Mart are to small merchants everywhere, namely, a huge threat to their survival. So too is Monsanto, the Darth Vader of genetically altered agriculture. Big farms, big buyers of agricultural products, and big farm suppliers are all antithetical to sustainable agriculture. If our food supply starts to shrink, or if the cost of food rises dramatically, then social and political upheaval are almost sure to follow

ANOMIE AND CONSUMERISM

For capitalism to work effectively, those who do the work must believe that the path to happiness involves accumulating enough money and credit so that they can purchase a nicely furnished home, a couple of cars, a computer, a home entertainment system, and a college education for their kids. To be able to afford all these things, they must work hard until they retire or die. The harder they work, the more money they will have, the more they can buy, and the happier they will be—so the story goes.

But if that were really true, why are so many people in the United States so anxious, so angry, so unhappy, so cynical, and so stressed out? Why are the rates of divorce, suicide, depression, abortion, substance abuse, and incarceration so high, if the American dream is working the way it's supposed to work? Why does the United States have the highest child-poverty rate of any industrial democracy? And why is that rate significantly higher than the rates found in Switzerland, Japan, Germany, and Sweden? Why are 6.6 million Americans either behind bars or on probation?

Although real per capita personal consumption expenditures nearly tripled over the last half century, the percentage of people claiming to be "very happy" actually declined by 5 percent. The Index of Social Health decreased by nearly 50 percent during the past quarter century.

Even though we live in a period of unprecedented prosperity, it is also the time of the *living dead*. Many affluent Americans who deny themselves virtually nothing in the way of material satisfaction seem to be more dead than alive. As novelist Walker Percy once said, "There is something worse than being deprived of life; it is being deprived of life and not knowing it."

The living dead can be found everywhere—surfing the Internet, checking their e-mail messages, blogging, daytrading, glued to Fox News hoping for an event in an otherwise uneventful life, driving alone across town to Wal-Mart in search of more low-priced plastic yuck, stopping at McDonald's for a quick taste-free meal, feigning interest in a mindless bureaucratic job, and viewing the saga of Anna Nicole Smith on TV. Our government, our politicians, and the high priests of corporate America pull our strings.

The defining characteristic of the American Empire is that ostensibly free individuals allow corporate America and the United States government to manipulate and control their lives through money, markets, media, and technology, resulting in the loss of political will, civil liberties, collective memory, and traditional culture.

Even though we all have different genetic maps, millions of Americans think the same, vote the same, watch the same TV programs, visit the same Web sites, and buy the same computer goods. Transnational megacompanies accountable to no one tell us what to buy, where we can work, how much we will be paid, and what the working conditions will be like. Like their state-run counterparts in the former Soviet Union, these giant companies are among the least democratic institutions in the world. They do everything possible to silence dissent and quell behavior which differs from the corporate norm. In these companies, there are no rights of freedom of speech, freedom of assembly, freedom of the press, or due process. One can be fired on the spot at the whim of one's supervisor. This is called "free enterprise."

For nearly a half century before the Soviet Union imploded in 1991, the Great Depression, World War II, and the Cold War provided our spiritual glue. However, after the demise of the Soviet Union, consumerism, technomania, and e-mania supplied the glue during the Clinton years. Since 11 September 2001, our nation has been consumed by the war on terrorism.

For how much longer can a society which behaves as though it were a community of corporate- and government-controlled robots, automatic devices which perform repetitive tasks in a seemingly human way, sustain itself morally, culturally, socially, and politically? We pretend to be "the captain of our ship and the master of our soul," even though we all march to the beat of the same drummers. We like to call it individualism; but some acute observers call it *technofascism*. How high a price are we prepared to pay to protect our energy-dependent consumerist lifestyle from the threat of terrorism? Are we willing to risk political and economic meltdown?

THE ENVIRONMENT

As Kirkpatrick Sale says, "Empires always end by destroying the lands and waters they depend on for survival, largely because they build and farm and grow without limits, and ours is no exception, even if we have yet to experience the worst of our assault on nature."

The environmental consequences of the American Empire are nearing disastrous levels at home: overmined mineral resources, overlogged forests, overcropped farm lands, overgrazed grasslands, overdrained wetlands, overtapped groundwaters, overfished seas, and overpolluted air and water. And, according to the Worldwatch Institute, these results have in turn given rise to climate change from greenhouse gas emissions, to extinction and loss of biodiversity, to forest loss, to decline in fisheries, and to scarcity of fresh water. Global warming has finally found its way onto the national radar screen.

With their unremitting commitment to growth and development at any cost, the high priests of corporate America have set out to Americanize the rest of the world. But can the world afford the environmental cost of being Americanized?

Although the U.S. accounts for only 5 percent of the world's population, it produces nearly a third of the global output and is responsible for a fourth of the deadly carbon dioxide buildup in the atmosphere— the principal cause of the greenhouse effect and global warming. This is in stark contrast to China, which contains 22 percent of the world's population but accounts for only 11 percent of the world's carbon dioxide. Carbon dioxide emissions per capita in Switzerland and Sweden are only one-third of those in the United States.

These figures are hardly surprising when you consider that the U.S. is either number one or near the top of the list of countries in the emission of air pollutants, per capita energy consumption, and the percentage of commuter trips made by private automobiles. Neither is it surprising that we import 60 percent of our daily consumption of oil, since the U.S. consumes 25 percent of the world's supply. As President Bush acknowledged in his 2006 State of the Union address, "America is addicted to oil."

Not only is the American Empire at risk, but the entire planet. In *Consuming Desires* Roger Rosenblatt estimates that "it would take three planets Earth to provide an American standard of living to the entire world. Yet it is that standard of living to which the whole world aspires." We must consider not just consumption of our resources, but also the waste that results when we are finished with them: the average American produces 1,646 pounds of waste per year.

Together China and India, two of the poorest countries in the world, have a combined population of 2.4 billion. Yet for years we have told them that they should be just like us. Unfortunately, they have decided to take us up on this suggestion with regard to the consumption of crude oil and other goods and services. With its population of 1.3 billion people, China has become the second largest oil-consuming country in the world. If present trends continue, China will surpass the United States within a few decades. Currently China imports over 40 percent of the oil it consumes. By 2025, China is expected to have to import 75 percent of its oil, and the U.S. 70 percent.

To satisfy its increasingly vociferous appetite for oil, China has embarked on a global strategy to acquire crude oil and oil-producing properties in Canada, the United States, Venezuela, and throughout Africa. China and Japan are skirmishing over offshore mineral rights in the South China Sea. A Chinese company tried unsuccessfully to acquire Unocal, one of the largest oil-producing companies in the U.S. It is only a matter of time before the United States and China will be engaged in a global showdown over the control of the world supply of crude oil. Although the U.S. Congress resisted the Chinese takeover bid for Unocal, China is not without some significant economic clout, since it owns a large portion of the U.S. government's foreign debt.

Neither the United Nations, the International Monetary Fund, the World Bank, the World Trade Organization, nor the European Union is committed to any other model of economic development than unlimited growth. Our government gives only lip service to environmental concerns while implementing one policy after another promoting free trade, unrestrained economic growth, and environmental degradation. One way to reduce air pollution in America would be to create public policies which lead to fewer cars on the road. A vibrant passenger railroad system would do just that. Yet, for all practical purposes, the United States has no passenger rail system outside of the Northeast Corridor between Washington, New York and Boston. Intercity passenger service in the rest of the country pales in comparison to the service found in Europe and Japan. And because of benign neglect by the Congress,

Amtrak teeters on the brink of bankruptcy most of the time. Much of the nation's infrastructure is obsolete and in need of repair—highways, bridges, tunnels, and electric power grids.

To add insult to injury, Team Bush called for reductions in the funding available through the Superfund program to clean up 33 of the most toxic waste sites in America. Among the sites earmarked for reduced funding was a plant in Edison, New Jersey which previously produced the herbicide Agent Orange. The administration also announced the most sweeping move in a decade loosening rules requiring oil refineries, power plants, and manufacturing plants to make costly investments in air pollution control equipment. And its approach to reductions in mercury emissions was tepid at best.

In a similar vein was a decision by a federal judge prohibiting Governor Jim Hodges from blocking government shipments of bomb-grade plutonium to the state of South Carolina. Against the will of the people of South Carolina, the Energy Department sought to move 6 ½ tons of plutonium to the Savannah River weapons installations site as part of its efforts to clean up and close its Rocky Flats weapons plant in Colorado.

Whether we are talking finite sources of crude oil, unrestrained economic growth, aging infrastructure, or inadequate environmental protection policies, the name of the game is the same—unsustainability, which leads to a high risk of economic, environmental, and political instability with potentially catastrophic results. Consider the case of Hurricane Katrina.

As far back as the early 1960s, when I was a graduate student at Tulane University, it was well known to local, state, and federal officials that New Orleans, the city that care forgot, was a catastrophe waiting to happen. A city nearly surrounded by water, several feet below sea level, protected only by a complex system of dams, levees, canals, and pumps, was a virtual time bomb.

When Category 4 Hurricane Katrina slammed ashore a few miles east of New Orleans with all its fury, the devastation was almost beyond belief. The following day, when the levee separating Lake Pontchartrain from New Orleans failed, flooding the City, only President George W. Bush seemed to have been surprised.

Katrina proved to be much more than just another hurricane; it represented an unprecedented direct hit to the belly of the beast, the American Empire. Not unlike 11 September 2001, Hurricane Katrina reminded us all of our vulnerability. The mayor of New Orleans, the governor of Louisiana, and the president of the United States were clueless as to how to respond to America's tsunami.

Tragic though it was, tens of thousands of New Orleanians, who either chose not to flee the City before Katrina struck, or could not do so, behaved as though they were experimental mice on an electric floor after experiencing learned helplessness from repeated shocks, waiting to be rescued by the City or the State, not knowing that the mayor and the governor had completely abdicated their responsibility for emergency assistance to the federal government. It was as though they were frozen in time in either the Superdome, the Convention Center, or on a stretch of Interstate 10. Unfortunately, the federal government was nowhere to be found until the fifth day after the storm. By the time the cavalry finally arrived, many were seriously ill, while others had died of neglect. It was too little, too late.

Who can ever forget the grim television images portraying New Orleans as an impoverished Third World country on the brink of anarchy? For nearly a week, thousands of mostly poor, African American New Orleanians were without food, water, shelter, medical care, and sanitary conveniences in the Louisiana heat, while Washington dithered. In addition to widespread looting there were fires, explosions, gunshots, murders, rapes, and robberies. All of this in the richest, most powerful nation in the world.

The U.S. government proved to be impotent to deal with the chaos generated by Hurricane Katrina. That it had so much difficulty coping with the aftermath of Katrina should have come as no surprise given its size and inflexibility.

To add insult to injury offers of economic and humanitarian assistance began pouring in from over 115 foreign countries including such economic powerhouses as Azerbaijan, Bangladesh, Cuba, Dominican Republic, Honduras, El Salvador and Sri Lanka. The Empire had been brought to its knees.

Just as politicians in New York began calling for the rebuilding of the World Trade Center almost immediately after 9/11, so too did President Bush call for the reconstruction of New Orleans, even before the rescue efforts were complete. No one asked why anyone in their right mind would want to rebuild New Orleans? So it could happen again?

The story of Katrina's rage against New Orleans is the story of too many people, crammed into too little space, who were too dependent on an ill-conceived flood control system and an impotent, unsustainable federal government which has lost its moral authority. The Department of Homeland Security is an oxymoron. One can only imagine its response to a nuclear or biological attack on a major American city such as New York, Washington, Chicago, or Los Angeles. The emperor truly has no clothes.

WHAT ARE OUR OPTIONS?

There is no more appropriate metaphor to illustrate the unsustainability of the United States than the events which took place on 11 September 2001. As I watched the two flaming 110-story towers of the World Trade Center crashing down to earth on live television, I had the eerie feeling that I was witnessing the collapse of the American equivalent of the Tower of Babel.

The Biblical account of the Tower of Babel is the story of a group of Israelites in ancient Babylon who, in defiance of God's will, built for themselves a city and a pyramid-shaped tower "with its top in the sky," so that they might make a name for themselves. The tower was grounded in hubris and the belief of its builders that they were bigger than life, truly invincible. They all spoke the same language and mistakenly thought there was no limit to what they might accomplish.

God was unamused by the tower and the Israelites' sense of unity and arrogance. By confusing their language, God effectively shut down their project and scattered them over the face of the earth.

Surely there were no more important icons of America's obsession with bigness, globalization, and imperialism than the World Trade Center and the Pentagon, the other terrorist target. The unmistakable phallic message of the twin towers could hardly have gone unnoticed—particularly by Third World nations, many of whom were innocent victims of globalization and American imperialism.

Why would anyone build two 110-story office buildings next to each other and then try to cram 50,000 people into them? Why would anyone consider rebuilding them? But that is exactly what most New Yorkers wanted. Each of the six proposals considered to rebuild the World Trade Center called for four to six new towers each of which would be 50 to 85 stories high. It's as though they still don't get it?

Just as the Israelites tried unsuccessfully to overcome their separation, meaninglessness, powerlessness, and fear of death by erecting the Tower of Babel, so too have Americans embraced consumerism, technomania, megalomania, globalization, and imperialism. In the words of William H. Willimon, former Dean of the Duke University Chapel, "In the process of perverted human attempts to unify and secure ourselves, we end up destroying ourselves, fracturing into a thousand different voices, falling to earth in disaster. Meltdown."

Our sense of outrage at the perpetrators of these heinous crimes stems not just from the human casualties and property losses, but from the deep psychological wounds inflicted upon all of us by the terrorists who managed to pierce the heart and soul of the home of the free and the brave. The wide-bodied jets which are alleged to have destroyed the World Trade Center towers and deeply penetrated the Pentagon were not only a challenge to American freedom and democracy, but also to our arrogance, omnipotence, and sense of invincibility.

Neither our economic, political, technological, nor military might could protect us from a handful of terrorists said to have been armed only with boxcutters and pen knives. After the crushing attack, all that remained of two once-proud New York edifices was a smoldering ash heap of glass, concrete, and steel, and the concomitant acrid smell. At least symbolically, we had been rendered impotent. There could be no doubt that we were indeed vulnerable. Our sustainability as a nation had been seriously challenged.

With a population of nearly 300 million people, the United States is the third largest nation in the world. But its megaeconomy dwarfs them all. The gross domestic product of the United States exceeds that of Japan, Germany, Britain, and France combined. If New York City were an independent nation-state its economy would rank fourteenth among the nations of the world.

But the September 11th terrorist attacks exposed the fact that big buildings, big businesses, big cities, big nations, and big military don't provide near the security we once thought. Like Eva Peron in the Broadway musical *Evita*, we "were supposed to have been immortal, but in the end [we] could not deliver."

Almost certainly, the United States is not sustainable forever as an empire, or even as a nation-state. And arguably its demise may be very near at hand. But while the clock is running, do we sit silently on the sidelines awaiting some apocalyptic economic, political, terrorist, or environmental event capable of bringing the house of cards crashing back to earth? Or do we consider alternatives to the "bigger is always better" model of supposed sustainability before the balloon gets so big that it pops? Do we go down with the Titanic, or do we seek other options, possibly even radical options, while options are still on the table?

What are the options available to us? The only ones I can envision are denial, compliance, political reform, implosion, rebellion, and dissolution.

Most Americans—including our government, our politicians, corporate America, Wall Street, the Pentagon, and the media—are in complete denial of our perilous plight. In spite of all of our obvious problems, they seem oblivious to the cataclysmic risks we are facing. But, obviously denial does not solve problems, and it seems clear that these problems will not simply vanish or solve themselves. So we reject this option.

Many armchair environmentalist, pacifist, democratic socialists, and simple-living adherents are all too aware of the risks facing the Empire, but feel completely powerless at the feet of corporate America and the U.S. government to do anything about them. So they talk about how bad things are and they try to live their personal lives in positive ways, but in relation to our government they do nothing but naively hope for the best. For them the name of the game is compliance. Since that gets us nowhere, we reject this option, too.

The real Pollyannas are liberal Democrats who believe that all we need do is elect the right Democrat president and all of our problems will be solved. They see political reform (such as campaign finance reform) as a panacea, failing to realize that, so long as the Congress is controlled by corporate America, there will never be any meaningful campaign finance reform. Since we have a single political party disguised as two, it matters not whether the president calls himself a Democrat or a Republican. The results will be the same. So, again, we reject this option.

When Soviet Leader Mikhail S. Gorbachev came to power in 1985, who could have imagined that the Soviet Union would soon implode and cease to exist? The United States seems to be well on its way to replicating the experience of its former archenemy in an American setting. So, do we want to sit by and wait for that to happen? Again, we reject this option.

That leaves the two options of rebellion or peaceful dissolution (which can also be named by the generally disfavored term "secession"). In the words of Kirkpatrick Sale,

> *So far the level of dissent within the U.S. has not reached the point of rebellion or secession—thanks both to the increasing repression of dissent and escalation of fear in the name of "homeland security" and to the success of our modern version of bread and circuses, a unique combination of entertainment, sports, television, internet sex and games, consumption, drugs, liquor, and religion that effectively deadens the general public into stupor.*

Just as armed rebellion gave birth to the United States in 1776, so too could some combination of stock market meltdown, economic depression, crippling unemployment monetary crisis, skyrocketing crude oil prices, double-digit interest rates, soaring federal deficits and trade imbalances, curtailment of social services, repeated terrorist attacks, return of the military draft or environmental catastrophe precipitate a violent twenty-first century revolution against corporate America and the U.S. government. However, we also reject this option, because we are opposed to all forms of violence.

There is, then, just one viable option: dissolution, which might plausibly be initiated by the secession of Vermont from the United States of America. Vermont provides a kinder, gentler, more communitarian alternative to a nation obsessed with money, power, size, speed, greed, and fear of terrorism. America needs a new model. Vermont stands ready to provide one. Secession represents the only morally defensible response to the American Empire.

We audaciously propose a radical new scenario for the United States. We imagine an America that follows the Vermont way and turns its vast national moral resources towards the creation of a new world *disorder* that makes the Vermont way accessible to the rest of the world—a disorder that rejects cant and dogma; a disorder that fosters creativity, possibility, and seething human enterprise; a disorder, most importantly, that promotes the decentralization of governance, beginning with an independent Republic of Vermont that delegates many of its powers down to the local level.

Chapter 2

VERMONT'S RADICAL IMPERATIVE

I love Vermont because of her hills and valleys, her scenery and invigorating climate, but most of all, because of her indomitable people. They are a race of pioneers who have almost beggared themselves to serve others. If the spirit of liberty should vanish in other parts of the union and support of our institutions should languish, it could all be replenished from the generous store held by the people of this brave little state of Vermont.

{ President Calvin Coolidge, 21 September 1928 }

Only in Vermont was the concept of a state as a self-constituted political community fully and radically tested... In this sense, Vermont was the only true American republic, for it alone has created itself.

{ Peter S. Onuf, *The Origins of the Federal Republic* }

Arguably Vermont is the most radical state in the Union in terms of its commitment to human solidarity, sustainability, direct democracy, egalitarianism, political independence, and nonviolence; and it's been that way for a long time. Its famous town meetings make the Green Mountain State second only to Switzerland as an international showcase for direct democracy. Not unlike Switzerland, Vermont's government works, and it works very well, for most of the people who live there.

Vermont's radicalism goes back at least to 15 January 1777, when it became an independent republic. It remained independent until it joined the Union as the fourteenth state on 4 March 1791. Because it was never a territory or colony belonging to some other government, it was the only American state which truly invented itself, an event which has left an indelible mark on the character of its citizens over two hundred years later.

Secession represents the most radical form of peaceful rejection of the policies of the central government a state can choose. Although Vermont is home to one of the most active political independence movements in the country today, there is absolutely nothing new about the notion of secession in Vermont. As far back as 5 January 1815, Vermont joined other New England states in signing the report of the so-called Hartford Convention in opposition to the proposal of the U.S. Secretary of War to implement a military draft for continuing the mismanaged

War of 1812 with England. This report was, indeed, a declaration of the right to secede.

In 1928 and 1929 a quirky little Vermont literary magazine known as The Drift-Wind published a series of tongue-in-cheek articles by Arthur Patton Wallace and Vrest Orton calling for Vermont independence. According to Orton, the purpose of such a movement would be "to constitute an Arcadia for persons of free thought, active mind, high standards, and aspirations and cultural imagination."

In 1973, Chicago-based economist David Hale, who grew up in St. Johnsbury, called for Vermont independence in a provocative piece in The Stowe Reporter entitled "The Republic of Vermont: A Modest Proposal." It won the New England Press Association Award that year.

In their town meetings in 1990, seven of seven independent-minded Vermont communities, including Montpelier and St. Johnsbury, voted overwhelmingly to secede from the Union. No one was surprised. A few years earlier when most Americans thought President Reagan could do no wrong, over 180 Vermont towns defied Reagan and demanded a nuclear freeze. Currently the town of Killington is trying to secede from Vermont and join New Hampshire. University of Vermont political scientist Frank Bryan says, "Vermont is just obstinate. We'll do anything to be on the wrong side." But is Vermont or America on the wrong side?

All three members of Vermont's Congressional delegation voted against the White House-backed resolution which gave President Bush the blessing of Congress to pursue military action against Iraq. Vermont was the only state in which every member of the delegation rejected the resolution. About the resolution Senator Patrick J. Leahy said, "This resolution permits the president to take whatever military action he wants, wherever he wants, for as long as he wants. It is a blank check… and this Vermonter does not sign blank checks."

At their 2005 town meetings fifty Vermont towns passed resolutions calling for the President and the Congress to take steps to withdraw all American troops from Iraq. Two years later both houses of the Vermont Legislature passed resolutions calling for the immediate withdrawal of all troops from Iraq—the first state legislature to do so. Thirty-six Vermont towns passed nonbinding resolutions in their 2007 town meetings demanding that President George W. Bush and Vice President Dick Cheney be impeached.

As part of Vermont's 1991 bicentennial celebration, Frank Bryan and Vermont Supreme Court Justice John Dooley traveled around the Green Mountain state debating the pros and cons of Vermont seceding from the Union. A few years earlier Bryan co-authored with Vermont State Representative Bill Mares a provocative little book entitled Out! The Vermont Secession Book. In this fantasy about the discovery of the Moscow Covenant – signed by George Washington and Ethan Allen – readers were led to the realization that Vermont never joined the Union, rather the Union joined Vermont; and "after two hundred years of bureaucracy, federal mismanagement, and un-Vermont-like actions, Vermont wants out." Most readers assumed that The Vermont Secession Book was written tongue-in-cheek. Others were not so sure when they read words like this:

> *Vermonters can do it better themselves. We are better at education, welfare, building roads, catching crooks, dispensing justice, and helping farmers. We report our own news better. Vermonters know much more about what's happening in Vermont than Americans know about what's happening in America. We're better at democracy, too, much better. We can balance our budget! We've watched as Congress pitters and patters, dillies and dallies, postures, poses, and primps. If that's America's idea of democracy, we want out!*

Dubbed "the patron saint of Vermont secession" by Frank Bryan and Bill Mares, David Hale proposed in a 6 January 2004 piece in The Burlington Free Press that Vermont become a tax haven and join the British Commonwealth. He wryly explained that one advantage of such a proposal would be the appearance in Montpelier of over fifty foreign embassies thus guaranteeing that on average there would be at least one good cocktail party in town each week.

More recently David Hale, Frank Bryan and over five hundred other Vermonters have come together to organize the Second Vermont Republic—a nonviolent citizens' network and think tank opposed to the tyranny of corporate America and the U.S. government and committed to the return of Vermont to its status as an independent republic and more broadly to the dissolution of the Union. Consistent with Vermont's radical imperative, the Second Vermont Republic embraces political independence, human scale, sustainability, economic solidarity, power sharing, equal opportunity, tension reduction, and mutuality.

A 2007 survey conducted by the Center for Rural Studies at the University of Vermont found that over thirteen percent of the eligible voters in Vermont now support secession making Vermont arguably the state with the highest percentage support for secession in the nation. Extrapolating from the survey to the entire state, there may be as many as 63,700 Vermonters who favor secession.

To put this thirteen percent figure in historical perspective, it is important to realize that when the thirteen English Colonies successfully seceded from the British Empire, only twenty-five percent of the population actually supported secession.

These results are hardly surprising when you consider the response of Vermont voters to a second question, namely, "Has the United States government lost its moral authority?" An astonishing 74.3 percent responded affirmatively. It was the loss of moral authority which brought down the apartheid government of South Africa, the communist regimes in six Eastern European countries, and the moribund Soviet Union.

Of those Vermonters who favor secession, 83.6 percent would like to see the question put before the 237 town meetings in the state. Ninety-three percent would then like to see the issue considered by the state legislature with 95.9 percent favoring a two-thirds majority of both houses for adoption.

From these initial observations one can see that Vermont is different from most states—very different. And many of these differences can be traced back to the life and times of Vermont's legendary folk hero Ethan Allen. In the eyes of some historians, Ethan Allen may have been the most underrated American revolutionary—a skilled military strategist, a patriot, a populist, a farmer, a businessman, a philosopher, and a writer—Vermont's equivalent of George Washington. But to others he was a belligerent, loud-mouthed, heavy-drinking, rebellious rabble-rouser—a charismatic charlatan, a braggart, an atheist, and a scoundrel with a strong penchant for political incorrectness. He both fought against and flirted with the British, and he was clearly more committed to creating an independent Vermont than to the creation of the United States (it was only after his death in 1789 that Vermont became the 14th state). Who was the real Ethan Allen? An American patriot, a traitor to his country, or a real Vermonter? Regardless of one's perspective, most agree he was truly bigger than life! About himself Allen said:

> *I was called by the Yorkers an outlaw, and afterwards, by the British, was called a rebel; and I humbly conceive, that there was as much propriety in the one name as the other.*

Whether Allen and his mythical Green Mountain Boys were outlaws, revolutionaries, or both, they seem to have embodied a great deal of the frontier spirit of their time. The northern frontier of New England was simultaneously democratic yet autocratic, egalitarian yet unjust, communitarian yet individualistic, and nonviolent yet militaristic. It fit with Frederick Jackson Turner's famous account of the American frontier in general:

> *The most important effect of the frontier has been in the promotion of democracy. The frontier is productive of individualism. Complex society is precipitated by the wilderness into a kind of primitive organization based on the family. The tendency is anti-social. It produces antipathy to control, and particularly to any direct control. The tax-gatherer is viewed as a representative of oppression.*

To the frontier the American intellect owes its striking characteristics. That coarseness and strength combined with acuteness and inquisitiveness; that practical, inventive turn of mind, quick to find expedients; that masterful grasp of material things, lacking in the artistic but powerful to effect great ends; that restless, nervous energy; that dominant individualism, working for good and evil, and with all that buoyancy and exuberance which comes with freedom—these are traits of the frontier.

These contradictions were all part and parcel of Ethan Allen, as well as part and parcel of the independent republic of Vermont. Is it possible that some of what Ethan Allen was up to in the divisive late eighteenth century may be worthy of emulation by independent-minded Vermonters in the twenty-first century?

THE GREEN MOUNTAIN MYSTIQUE

Poet Robert Frost, who spent his summers in a cabin near Middlebury College's Bread Loaf Campus, captured the essence of Vermont in his poem "The Road Not Taken":

Two roads diverged in a wood, and I –
Took the one less traveled by,
And that has made all the difference.

Every visitor to Vermont is struck by the majestic beauty of Vermont's Green Mountains, not unlike the Swiss, Bavarian, and Austrian Alps: the classic red barns, the covered bridges, the picturesque patchwork pattern of small farms, black-and-white Holsteins, tiny villages, little rivers, ridges, hollows, and dirt roads, and the fact that there are no billboards. Because they like it that way, Vermonters have the highest percentage of unpaved roads in the country. Not surprisingly, roadside billboards were banned in 1968.

Nestled between Lake Champlain in the west and the Connecticut River in the east, and between Massachusetts to the south and Canada to the north, Vermont ranks 43rd in land mass and 49th in population among the 50 states.

Two important factors contribute to Vermont's uniqueness—its tiny size (one fiftieth the population of California) and the fact that it is by far the most rural state in America. With 72.2 percent of its 623,000 inhabitants living in the countryside, Vermont stands in sharp contrast to the nation as a whole, which is only 19.7 percent rural. Only West Virginia with a 70 percent rural population even comes close to Vermont.

To put Vermont's size in perspective, eight of the ten richest countries in the world are tiny European states—Luxembourg, Norway, Switzerland, Denmark, Iceland, Liechtenstein, Sweden, and Ireland. Five of them have higher per capita incomes than the United States, and all eight have lower incidences of poverty, drug abuse, violence, and crime than the U.S. They also have less pollution, less traffic congestion, and less urban sprawl than we have. Three of them—Luxembourg with a population of 469,000, Liechtenstein with 34,000, and Iceland with 297,000—are actually smaller than Vermont.

In Vermont there are no cities, no big buildings, few shopping malls, no military bases, few big businesses, few homicides, virtually no gun control laws, and no waiting lines. In addition, there is almost no traffic congestion, little indigenous air pollution, and no death penalty.

The harsh Vermont winters are colder, darker, and longer than those found in most places in the United States: the annual snowfall often exceeds ten feet.

Life is lived at a slower, more deliberate, more casual pace in the Green Mountain state. Vermonters are not in nearly such a big hurry as their nearby neighbors in New York, New Hampshire, Massachusetts, and Quebec. Theirs is a live-and-let-live lifestyle: they are not intent on sticking their noses in everybody else's business.

Compared to many, Vermonters are more caring, less greedy, less aggressive, less competitive, more tolerant, and less infected with affluenza—the obsessive-compulsive consumption of more and more stuff. In Vermont one finds a commitment to the land, to history, to culture, and to the environment. Civic responsibility is still alive and well.

In summary, what makes Vermont work is that it is tiny, rural, radical, and green, the combination of which gives it enormous energy.

FREEDOM AND UNITY

It was not by chance alone that "Freedom and Unity" became the state's motto. Only Vermont and Texas were independent republics before joining the Union. Unlike the other New England states, Vermont was never an English colony thus avoiding a period of aristocratic oligarchy. Influenced by some of its earlier Iroquois and Yankee inhabitants, Vermont established an almost casteless society never to be replicated elsewhere in America.

As early as 2 July 1777, the Constitution of Vermont presciently anticipated the risks of the future military-industrial complex by stating:

> *That the people have a right to bear arms for the defence of themselves and the State—and as standing armies in time of peace are dangerous to liberty, they ought not to be kept up; and that the military should be kept under strict subordination to and governed by the civil power.*

Vermont has for the most part avoided wars in its territory, through-out its history. No major battle between European invaders and Native Americans ever took place in Vermont territory. Although Ethan Allen's Green Mountain Boys had no love for New Yorkers or the British, both they and Allen himself managed to avoid ever killing anyone at Fort Ticonderoga or elsewhere – so the story goes. Only one minor skirmish occurred on Vermont soil during the American Revolution. And the lone Civil War engagement fought in Vermont—on 18 October 1864 in St. Albans—was more like a Jesse James-style bank robbery, carried out by a handful of Confederate soldiers.

Although Ethan Allen was certainly no pacifist, he may have been a better actor than a soldier. He often made use of threatening gestures as an alternative to violence and played heavily on the element of surprise while bringing large numbers to bear against an unsuspecting enemy. He liked to keep his options open, including the possibility of retreat.

Even though there are only three thousand African Americans living in Vermont, thus making it the state with the smallest black population by percentage, Vermont does have an exemplary civil rights record. No blacks were ever imported to pick cotton or anything else in Vermont. Nor were they ever shunted into urban industrial ghettoes in Vermont; indeed, there are no such ghettoes in Vermont.

Vermont was the first state to outlaw slavery in its constitution, already in 1777 when it was created as an independent republic; and it was also the first to require universal manhood suffrage. By the 1830s, Vermont had the strongest abolitionist sentiment of any state in America. Vermonters were active participants in the "Underground Railroad" which helped runaway slaves find refuge in Canada. In 1858, in defiance of the Federal Fugitive Slave Law, Vermont formally freed all blacks who had been brought into the state. In 1861 Vermont was the first state to send troops to fight in the Civil War, and half of the eligible men in Vermont served in the Union Army.

Although African Americans were few in number, several black Vermonters have distinguished themselves, as far back as the nineteenth century. For example, Alexander Twilight became the first black to earn a college degree when he graduated from Middlebury College in 1823; and when he was elected to the Vermont legislature in 1836, Mr. Twilight became the first black legislator in America. He was followed by George Washington Henderson, who graduated from the University of Vermont in 1877 at the top of his class—the second black to become a member of the national honor society Phi Beta Kappa.

Idaho, Montana, North Dakota, South Dakota, and Wyoming also have few blacks, for the same reasons one finds in Vermont. When the mass out-migration of blacks from the South began in the 1930s and continued into the 1970s, southern blacks were drawn to large industrial cities in the North where the best jobs were. African Americans have never been attracted to regions which have winters such as those found in places like Montana and Vermont—particularly if few jobs were to be found there. But those who did find their way to Vermont have been welcomed and fully included.

Vermont is recognized internationally for the unique form of direct democracy practiced by 237 of its 246 towns. In these towns, the executive is a three- to five-member board of selectmen, and the legislative branch is literally the annual town meeting which is held on the first Tuesday in March each year. Although the format is a little different in Burlington, Rutland, Brattleboro, and six other large towns, their governments are strongly democratically based too. So important is Town Meeting Day that when Jim Douglas became Vermont's governor in 2003, he continued to serve as moderator at the Middlebury town meeting.

Professor Frank Bryan spent 34 years collecting data from 1,669 Vermont town meetings to produce the definitive work on town meetings, entitled Real Democracy. Bryan argues that real democracy requires:

> First, governments small enough to give a significant number of citizens a significant chance to make a significant difference on a significant number of issues. Second, larger governments that trust their citizens enough to let them make mistakes on matters of importance.

He calls for a radical reordering of public and private power downward—a paradigm reversal.

> Let us ask first: is this government small enough and not is this government big enough? Let us ask first: can this store deliver goods humanly and not can this store deliver goods efficiently? Let us ask first: does this school understand its community and not does this school understand how to give exams?

Whether we are talking independence, nonviolence, the treatment of blacks, or direct democracy, Vermont has always led the way in America. Its longstanding radicalism goes very deep.

THE VERMONT FAMILY FARM

The family farm still represents the very essence of the Vermont mystique. Not surprisingly, the statue atop the Vermont State House is that of Ceres, the patroness of agriculture, rather than either Vulcan, the patron of manufacturing, or Mercury, who might be loosely construed to be the patron of tourism.

Although Vermont farm income is $650 million dollars, total agri-business income including ice cream, cheese, chocolates, specialty meats, maple sugar houses, and farm tours is estimated to be close to $3 billion. Over 50,000 people are employed in agri-business.

However, there are now only 6,000 farms left in Vermont, of which only 1,000 or so are dairy farms, whereas in 1950 there were over 11,000 dairy farms alone. Globalization, reduced federal milk subsidies, bovine growth hormones, giant corporate farms out West, oversupply, and the rising cost of technology have driven hundreds of Vermont dairy farmers off the land.

Long before Vermont became an independent republic in 1777, Native Americans and European settlers in the area began making high-quality maple sugar. Since there was little or no white sugar available in New England, maple sugar became a staple. In 1793, for example, sugarmakers in the town of Cavendish made 80,000 pounds of maple sugar—all produced outdoors, over open fires, in iron kettles.

So important is maple sugarmaking in Vermont that the sugaring season begins each year with the Governor's Official Tree Tapping Ceremony. This ceremony also signals the beginning of "Maple Open House Weekend," a statewide promotion of maple products and related events.

Over one hundred sugarhouses statewide participate in the Maple Open House Weekend. Sugarhouse visitors have the opportunity to observe tapping and boiling while sampling maple syrup, maple cream, maple candy, Indian sugar, cotton candy, maple donuts, and sugar-on-snow. Over three dozen country inns, B&Bs, and restaurants also participate in the Maple Open House.

Every Halloween for over 25 years, Billy and Karen Moynihan have presented a Jack-o-lantern show at Ellie's Farm Market near Northfield. The show consists of 1,000 hand-carved, lighted pumpkins scattered around the grounds in the woods near the farm market. The family and a few friends carve the pumpkins for the show, offered to the community as thanks for supporting their seasonal farm business. Folks donate to defray costs, but the Moynihans give all contributions to a different charity each year.

Vermont's $4 billion tourist industry is strongly influenced by visual images of the countryside sprinkled with red barns, rolling meadows, and black-and-white Holsteins. Values such as independence, self-sufficiency, democracy, resourcefulness, hard work, perseverance, and a strong sense of community can be traced directly to the family farm. Without these values there would be no Vermont.

In their book *The Vermont Papers*, Frank Bryan and John Mc-Claughry described the Vermont farmer as follows:

> For all Vermonters it is the farmer (along with logger and quarryman) who produces closest to the land. Historically, during the centuries when agricultural life gave form and substance to

Vermont, the farmer was not a party to the manipulation of paper values and the realization of windfall gains, or to a life without hard physical work in such conditions as the changing seasons would provide. His was the world of the genuine, the natural, the God-given. He arose before dawn, conformable to the needs of his livestock. He savored the pungent aroma of the cow barn, the fragrance of the apple blossoms in May, the smell of the new-mown hay. He and his farm wife planned their life together to do what had to be done, cutting wood for the winter and the sugaring, fixing fence, seeing the milk safely to the dairy, guiding their son's hands for the first time he steered team or tractor, putting up food for the long winters. Affluent the farmer was not, but strong in mind and spirit, an essential working part of a beautiful though sometimes severe world which made sense – and was profoundly satisfying– to those who dwelt within it.

Although it's easy to overromanticize the Vermont family farm, it would be hard to overemphasize its contributions to Vermont's independence, sense of community, environmental consciousness, and radical politics. It's hard to imagine what Vermont might be like if it were just another urban industrial megastate. Would it be able to avoid urban poverty, homelessness, crime, congestion, sprawl, traffic jams, pollution, and a complete breakdown of community? I think not. Vermont farms are small and now fairly few in number, but still they provide the glue which makes the whole state work. The importance of their survival cannot be overstated.

VERMONT COMMUNITY LIFE

Although the backwoods isolation of Vermont's hills and valleys fosters self-sufficiency, it also provides a breeding ground for real community and a radical politics seldom found in America. From the outset, the combination of the harsh winters and the small farms, villages, and towns has engendered a variety of communal activities including barn-raisings, work bees, electric co-ops, and—more recently—cohousing and intentional communities. From *The Vermont Papers* we learn:

Vermont is a place of ups and downs. Its land seems to cluster people in little communities by nature. The winters are cold, the coldest in New England. The snow comes early and lasts and lasts and lasts. The soil is rocky, the living tough. Vermont's geography contains a dual imperative: it cradles settlements and it makes living difficult. So Vermonters, harkening to humankind's basic need for cooperation, come to huddle like the Swiss in small communities, mountain towns and villages. They seek the safety of

unity, of Congregationalism, of neighbor, church and town. Their
spirits crave liberty, but the land compels union.

Vermont is a state full of towns and villages, not cities. Its largest town, Burlington, has a population of only 40,000. Among the better known Vermont towns are Bennington, Brattleboro, Middlebury, and Rutland, with populations ranging from 5,000 to 20,000. But many of the towns in Vermont are considerably smaller than that.

Community is still alive and well in many of the towns and villages of Vermont – in places like Bristol, Chelsea, Ludlow, Newport, Peacham, and Quechee, to mention only a few. Although we have not been able to come up with a prescriptive formula for a successful Vermont community, there are some common elements shared by many Vermont villages – a town hall, a school, a library, a Congregationalist Church, a post office, a country inn, and several stores, including a general store. The traditional Vermont general store was an early precursor to the shopping mall. In the not-too-distant past, it was common for a general store to include a grocery store, an apothecary, a post office, a pub, a barbershop, and a doctor's office. More often than not, it was some combination of the general store, the town meeting, the village school, and the local church which provided the sense of community for a Vermont village.

Each year as many as 20,000 people are drawn to the funky, grassroots, seat-of-the-pants Fourth of July Parade in the tiny village of Warren in the Mad River Valley. The parade, whose homemade floats are held together by duct tape and baling twine, has no marching bands, only bands that march. The parade combines New England Americana with vintage Vermont culture and the residual effects of 1960s hippie culture. Many of the floats reflect the radical imperative of those living in the Mad River Valley.

The parade begins at ten o'clock sharp, rain or shine, just south of the covered bridge over the Mad River. It then winds its way down Main Street past the Town Hall, the Post Office, the fire station, the Warren United Church, the Warren Country Store, and the posh Pitcher Inn. (It's worth a trip to Warren just to have lunch at the Warren Store along the banks of Kid's Creek.) The parade turns right up Brooks Road then meanders up School Road to Brooks Field adjacent to the Warren Elementary School, where parade-goers enjoy live music, bake sales, barbecue, craft exhibits, and field games. Over the years, parade fans have indulged in pony rides, horse pulls, nickel a pitch, baseball toss, dart games, helicopter rides, and pie throwing. There is usually dancing in the village as well.

In addition to a wide variety of unique floats, the parade may include fire trucks, motorcycles, covered wagons, the Warren hearse, walking bands, riding bands, as well as various farm animals. The parade is led by a parade marshal, often dressed in a spiffy parade uniform. As the parade passes the judges' stand each float pauses for a few seconds so that it can be considered for one of the many parade prizes: best in parade, most patriotic, best commercial, best children's, best car, best bike, best horse-drawn vehicle, most original, most imaginative, best antique auto, and funniest. A summer visit to Vermont is incomplete if you don't experience Warren's "Famous Fantastic Old Fashioned Fourth."

Another not-to-be-missed summer event which draws large crowds in Central Vermont is the Thunder Road International Speed Bowl in Barre. The quarter-mile, high-banked, asphalt, oval stock car racing track is considered to be one of the top short tracks in America. Because of the number of Franco-American drivers, Thunder Road is very popular with French-Canadians and Vermonters alike. Anyone running for statewide public office in Vermont must be seen occasionally at Thunder Road.

Chicken pie dinners, church socials, peace demonstrations, pot smoking, intentional communities, Fourth of July parades, and NASCAR races are all part of what underlies Vermont's unique, radical, rural culture.

THE SOUND OF MUSIC

When Julie Andrews mesmerized millions with her lilting lyrics as she sang "The hills are alive with the sound of music," she was singing about the Austrian Alps surrounding Salzburg. But she might very well have been singing about Vermont's Green Mountains, which have far more in common with their taller Austrian counterparts than many realize.

Salzburg was the home of Baron Von Trapp and his seven children who, along with his young bride Maria, fled Austria in the 1930s before it was overrun by the Nazis. Eventually settling in Vermont, the Von Trapps started the popular Trapp Family Singers and opened the Trapp Family Lodge in idyllic Stowe.

As with Austria and Switzerland, dozens of Vermont towns have some sort of country fair or festival each summer. One can spend the entire summer attending festivals ranging from the European-style Vermont Mozart Festival to the Quechee hot-air balloon festival, the Bread and Puppet Circus, and the Tunbridge World's Fair. A typical festival is the week-long Middlebury Festival on the Green, in which friends and neighbors are treated to a variety of different types of music each evening – classical, jazz, international, bluegrass, and Cajun.

When the Mozart Festival was started in 1974, it was envisioned as a joint celebration of the creative genius of Wolfgang Amadeus Mozart and the natural beauty of Vermont, which is so similar to Mozart's Salzburg. (Coincidentally, Mozart's short life ended in 1791, the year Vermont became the fourteenth state of the United States: Mozart was a contemporary of Ethan Allen.) Each summer the Mozart Festival holds 15 to 20 concerts at a variety of scenic sites scattered throughout the Champlain Valley and the Green Mountains. Festival concerts in the coachyard and the formal gardens of Shelburne Farms are a reminder of other courtyards and royal gardens where Mozart performed in Europe in the eighteenth century.

It's hard to imagine a more pleasurable experience than sitting on the lawn of the Shelburne Farms Inn, enjoying a summer picnic and listening to a South Porch concert as the sun sets over Lake Champlain in the Adirondacks and the moon rises over the Green Mountains. Each year several thousand Vermonters and out-of-state guests enjoy not only the beautiful music of Mozart, Beethoven, Bach, Chopin, Handel, Strauss, and others, but also a sense of community and a sense of connectedness to the land, the environment, and the music of our European ancestors.

The Festival taps into the heart and soul of Vermont and encourages us to fantasize about what the Green Mountains might become, if they too were alive with the sights and sounds of Salzburg, Innsbruck, Geneva, or St. Moritz. Could it be that the Mozart Festival is much more than just a summer musical delight? Is it not a window of opportunity through which the future might flow – a vision of what Vermont might someday become?

Burlington, one of the most sophisticated small towns in America, is the heart and soul of the Vermont music scene. In addition to a dozen or so clubs with nightly live music, the acoustically perfect Flynn Center provides a plethora of world-class performing arts events throughout the year. And Burlington's annual First Night festival creates a community-based, alcohol-free New Year's Eve celebration of the performing arts. Participants can pick and choose among dozens of different musical events and performances scattered all over town in colleges, schools, theaters, churches, and auditoriums. Over 20,000 people participate each year.

On most Wednesday nights when the Vermont legislature is in session, one can catch a lively act in the chamber of the House of Representatives in the Statehouse in Montpelier. Known as "Farmers' Night at the Statehouse," these weekly performances date back to the Vermont Farmers' Club in the 1920s. During the early years, the Farmers' Club meetings took the form of public forums devoted primarily to the concerns of Vermont farmers—at that time, most members of the legislature were farmers who spent the entire legislative week in Montpelier, since neither roads nor transportation were conducive to commuting.

But the purchase of a piano by the club in 1923 signaled the beginning of a gradual shift of emphasis away from lectures and public discussions towards a format that included more and more entertainment. That same year the club relaxed its membership requirements so that any representative "interested in the soil" could be a member of the Vermont Farmers' Club. On a typical Wednesday evening one may enjoy a concert by a local high school or college musical group, a barbershop quartet, the 40th Army Band, or the Vermont Symphony Orchestra. By far, the most interesting meeting the Farmers' Club ever had took place on 26 March 1947, when Representative Reide LeFevre brought his own circus to the Statehouse. The circus included a calliope, a cowboy band, roller-skating, acrobatics, knife throwing, and nearly everything connected with a carnival. There were also horses and elephants. Nearly a thousand people showed up that night. *Life Magazine* covered the story.

The most unique and the most politically radical festival in Vermont is Our Domestic Resurrection Circus, performed weekly each July and August by the Bread and Puppet Theater. Each summer several thousand pilgrims find their way to a remote abandoned gravel pit, now used as an amphitheater, near the tiny village of Glover in the Northeast Kingdom of Vermont. There they are treated to a free outdoor puppet circus complete with sideshows, music, pageant, and delicious free homemade German sourdough rye bread made personally by Bread and Puppet founder, producer, director, writer, actor, musician, artist, and sculptor Peter Schumann. Through the use of bigger-than-life human puppets the puppeteers confront such issues as affluenza, technomania, megalomania, robotism, globalization, imperialism, war, poverty, and hunger. Many of the shows are grounded in a combination of radical politics and liberation theology. There is an excellent book of essays and photographs on Bread and Puppet by Ronald T. Simon and Marc Estrin entitled Rehearsing With Gods, which examines eight recurring themes of Bread and Puppet performances—Death, Fiend, Beast, Human, World, Gift, Bread, and Hope.

On a somewhat less esoteric level, there are dozens of country fairs scattered all over Vermont each summer, of which the Tunbridge World's Fair is probably the best known. This legendary fair has been around since 1861 and got its nickname from a politician's bombast back in its rowdier days. Each June 10,000 people visit the Tunbridge Fairgrounds for the two-day Vermont History Expo. The event is sponsored by the Vermont Historical Society, in collaboration with the 175 local historical societies scattered throughout the state of Vermont. The colorful gathering features a broad array of historians, re-enactors, genealogists, performers, musicians, and craftsmen who are actively involved in telling the state's stories. These stories highlight the unique and rich heritage of Vermont which makes it a special place to live, work, and visit.

The Vermont Mozart Festival, Burlington's First Night, Farmers' Night at the Statehouse, Bread and Puppet, and the Tunbridge World's Fair are, to be sure, about entertainment and music; but they are also about Vermont's sense of community, its connectedness, its creativity, its self-sufficiency, its culture, and its humanity. These festivals, fairs, and performances contribute to the sense of meaning and purpose of thousands of ordinary Vermonters. They also reflect Vermont's uniqueness—a uniqueness which few Vermonters are willing to have subsumed by corporate America, the U.S. government, and globalization.

THE KINGDOM

Although I had visited Glover's Bread and Puppet Theater and passed through St. Johnsbury and Newport en route to Quebec, I had never really experienced Vermont's mythical Northeast Kingdom until I encountered Essex County's infamous Victory Bog.

After passing Victory, a town consisting of two dilapidated, uninhabited houses, I drove for nearly ten miles through the isolated, fogenshrouded bog without passing a car or seeing a single soul along the spooky dirt road. Even though Victory Bog is only ten miles from St. Johnsbury, it was as if I had stepped back in time over a hundred years into another world – a world of solitude, stillness, and silence.

As I stood surrounded by the eerie silence, I wondered what it was like back in the days of Ethan Allen when there was no electricity and no indoor plumbing, not to mention automobiles, interstate highways, shopping malls, fast-food restaurants, Wal-Marts, or union high schools. How did one survive without television, cell phones, fax machines, computers, and the Internet?

As I left the bog en route to the picturesque upper Connecticut River Valley, I passed tiny Gallup Mills, Granby's one-room school house, and Guildhall's quaint little courthouse. After a great lunch at Jennifer's Café in Island Pond, across the street I discovered Simon the Tanner, a charming shoe shop operated by the apocalyptic religious sect known as The Community.

Not far away, in Barnet, is a quite different kind of spiritual center, the 540-acre Karme Chöling Buddhist Meditation Center. With its striking beauty and live-and-let-live ambiance, the Kingdom is home to a plethora of artists, writers, and musicians. Vermont's French Connection is nurtured there as well.

One sees a lot of "Take Back Vermont" signs in the Kingdom – code for those opposed to Vermont's first-in-the-nation Civil Union law. But many of the beneficiaries of this law also reside there. The Civil Union law is but one of many examples of Vermont's tolerance and live-and-let-live lifestyle. For those who have wondered, "What ever happened to all the hippies of the 1960s?" I suggest this answer: A heck of a lot of them seem to be living in Vermont.

Some of the members of the Second Vermont Republic would liked to co-opt the "Take Back Vermont" slogan and use it not for gay-bashing but rather for bashing the American Empire. They would like to Take Back Vermont from corporate America and the U.S. government. As the Empire becomes ever more repressive and ever less stable, it is only a matter of time before Take Back Vermonters realize that their real enemy is the Empire, not gays and lesbians.

Otherwise, life in the Kingdom tends to be even more laid back than in the rest of Vermont. Small is still beautiful, and with the exception of the sound of chain saws whining in the distance in the woods, it's a lot quieter too.

There is also a sense of tragedy in the Northeast Kingdom. Many of the stately red barns, once the pride of prosperous dairy farmers, are not only idle but have fallen into complete disrepair. Some are near collapse—a vivid reminder of the demise of the family farm. A quick trip through the countryside will confirm that life can be tough in the Kingdom. It is the poorest, least developed region in the state. Substance abuse, child abuse, and sexual abuse are problems in the Kingdom. A lot of pot is grown and smoked there.

Although St. Johnsbury has a number of big box retail stores, the Kingdom has no Wal-Mart. But there is one just across the river in Littleton, New Hampshire, which has no sales tax. There are few remaining small merchants in the Kingdom, with the few concentrated in Lyndonville, Newport and St. Johnsbury. One well-placed Wal-Mart between Lyndonville and St. Johnsbury would probably take out all those that remain.

Not surprisingly, since the Kingdom is by far the most radical part of Vermont, all of the early meetings of the Second Vermont Republic were held there: the Lake Parker Country Store in West Glover was once considered to be our power base. Even though the Northeast Kingdom is considered by some to be the only real Vermont, it suffers from neglect by Montpelier and the rest of the state. But without the Kingdom, Vermont would not be Vermont. Vermont needs the Kingdom a lot more than the Kingdom needs the rest of Vermont.

HUNTING MOOSE NOT HOMO SAPIENS

The sixteen most dangerous days in the Green Mountain state each year are the deer hunting season. On the other hand, Vermont's gun control laws are among the most lax in the nation; Vermonters are into shooting deer and moose, rather than each other.

The experience of Vermont casts some doubt on the popular American myth that the only way to fight crime is through tougher law enforcement and increased criminal justice expenditures. In spite of the fact that it spends considerably less than the national average per capita for criminal justice, Vermont consistently ranks at the top of the list of least violent states in the nation. No one has been executed by the state of Vermont since the 1950s, and the percentage of the population incarcerated is among the lowest in the nation. Several years ago in

Richmond, Virginia – a city of 200,000 inhabitants – there were 160 homicides. During that same year Vermont, which has a population three times the size of Richmond, had only five homicides.

Vermont's penchant for nonviolence may have been influenced by none other than Ethan Allen. Allen often used his rather considerable oratorical skills to confront rich and powerful land owners on behalf of poor, independent farmers and small communities. He put pressure on the British, but he also strongly and effectively opposed wealthy land speculators intent on stealing the land of yeoman farmers. By empowering the powerless without using violence, Allen helped Vermont invent itself as an independent republic. Long before the power of nonviolence was popularized by M.K. Gandhi, Martin Luther King Jr., Lech Walesa, and Vaclav Havel, Ethan Allen demonstrated an uncanny understanding of the power of the powerless.

In spite of Vermont's history of nonviolence and resistance to militarization, on any given day one can see up to 20 gas-guzzling F-16 fighter jets flying in and out of the Burlington International Airport. Not only do these screaming cold war relics endanger the lives of hundreds of commercial airline passengers each day, but they also fly at dangerously low altitudes over Burlington and the University of Vermont campus. At $20 million a pop, the F-16s are the pride of the modern-day "Green Mountain Boys," the Vermont Air National Guard unit named after Ethan Allen's pre-Revolutionary minutemen volunteers.

But now that the cold war is over, from whom are these F-16s protecting Vermont? Why on earth would anyone want to invade tiny Vermont? Vermont has no military bases, no large cities, no important government installations, and no strategic resources unless you count one aging nuclear power plant. What if Canada, China, Russia, North Korea, Iran, or even the U.S. Marines were to invade the Green Mountain state? Just what would they do with it? Would all of the black-and-white Holsteins be confiscated, or perhaps the entire sugar maple crop be burned? Imagine trying to enslave freedom-loving Vermonters. Good luck!

Vermont is too small, too rural, and too independent to be invaded by anyone. It is a threat to no one. Furthermore, Vermonters, not unlike the Swiss, tend to stick to their own knitting rather than intruding into the affairs of their neighbors. Vermont has always been that way and probably always will be.

After the 11 September 2001 terrorist attacks on the World Trade Center, Vermont's F-16s began providing protective cover for New York City. Hopefully, someday soon they will be reassigned to a military base closer to New York. Vermont has no more need for violence on a military level than it has for violence on a personal level.

The Vermont Way of Politics

In an unexpected David and Goliath encounter led by Senator James M. Jeffords, the Vermont Way – political independence and social conscience – trumped what President George W. Bush calls the American Way of Life.

By splitting with the Republican Party, becoming a Vermont Independent, and precipitating a major political power shift in Congress, Jeffords was following a long tradition of freedom and independence going all the way back to the days of Ethan Allen and his Green Mountain Boys. In the speech announcing his departure from the Republican Party, Jeffords cited a number of other compassionate, independent Republican politicians from Vermont, including President Calvin Coolidge and Senator George Aiken.

Until recently, Vermont was traditionally a Republican state, but this was neither the mean-spirited Republicanism found in New Hampshire nor the racially based Republicanism so common in the South. Vermont politics is a politics of reason. It avoided the anticommunist hysteria generated by McCarthyism in the 1950s, and it has been spared the destructive consequences of the politics of race.

As evidence of the political independence of Vermonters, consider the 2004 election. Moderate Republican Governor Jim Douglas and his conservative running mate Lt. Governor Brian Dubie carried Vermont by a substantial majority, as did liberal Democratic presidential candidate John Kerry, moderate Democratic Senator Patrick J. Leahy, and Progressive Congressman Bernie Sanders. Party label did not make a whit of difference.

Even today the undeniable effects of the politics of Ethan Allen can still be found in Vermont. Allen learned a great deal about negotiation and psychological warfare from the nearby Iroquois Indians. For example, just as the Iroquois kept the British and French in suspense as to which side they would support during much of the eighteenth century, so too did Ethan Allen play off the British and the United States against each other during Revolutionary times. He understood that by manipulating an enemy's fears and desires the need for violence can be reduced. He successfully employed this philosophy to create and preserve Vermont's independence—and independent is the way Vermonters still want to be.

Not only are Vermonters radically independent politically, but they have a different take on economics as well. They have traditionally been willing to tax themselves heavily to provide high-quality public schools, child care, early childhood education, medical care, mental health services, and social welfare services. Vermonters are careful with their money and they like to keep it local: Vermont was one of two states which did not experience bank closures during the early 1930s, and one of three states in which there were no savings and loan bank failures in the 1980s.

Furthermore, Vermonters prefer to keep their governments small and responsive. Vermont is one of only two states which have a two-year term for governor. Montpelier, Vermont's tiny state capital with a population of 8,035, is the nation's smallest, and there is no traditional governor's mansion in Montpelier. As Bryan and McClaughry put it in The Vermont Papers, Vermont politics is "a politics of human scale [which] can give expression to humankind's longed-for ideals of liberty and community, freedom and unity."

CAN WE KEEP VERMONT GREEN AND "UNDEVELOPED"?

Long before it became fashionable to do so, many Vermonters maintained a high level of environmental consciousness. This is evinced by the 385,000-acre Green Mountain National Forest, the state's 33 parks and recreational areas, the 270-mile Long Trail which winds its way from Massachusetts to the Canadian border, and the fact that virtually every one of Vermont's 246 towns has a well-kept village green in the center of town. In 1936 the people of Vermont soundly rejected a proposal by the federal government to construct a Green Mountain Parkway similar to the Blue Ridge Parkway.

Nevertheless, by 1970 real estate development had produced such adverse effects in Vermont that the legislature passed an unprecedented law aimed at controlling the abuse of Vermont's natural heritage—Act 250. According to Act 250, any substantial public or private real estate development project must obtain a permit certifying that the project will not adversely affect air and water quality, water supplies, roads and transportation, public schools, municipal services, scenic beauty, historic sites, wildlife, and irreplaceable natural areas.

Even this stronger effort has not been completely effective. Sub-urban sprawl has turned the ten-mile stretch of Route 7 south of Burlington into a strip-mall as unsightly as that of any large American city. What was once a scenic drive near Lake Champlain to the quaint village of Shelburne has managed to attract a plethora of fast-food restaurants, automobile dealerships, discount stores, and shopping malls. During most of the day there is bumper-to-bumper traffic between Burlington and Shelburne. Brattleboro and Rutland also have unseemly strip malls.

Certainly there are counteracting forces and activities that continue to work against this trend. The University of Vermont, Middlebury College, and Sterling College all have excellent programs in environmental studies. The Vermont Law School in South Royalton is considered to have the strongest environmental law program in the nation.

In spite of these efforts, in May 2004 the National Trust for Historic Preservation designated the entire state of Vermont as one of America's eleven most "endangered historical places"—the second time the state had been placed on the list. That Vermont, of all states, would end up on this endangered species list took many people by surprise, since it was the first state to ban billboards and the second to enact a bottle-deposit law. On both occasions it was above all the state's assault by Wal-Mart that resulted in its being placed on such an inauspicious list. Since the days of Ethan Allen, Vermont has always been different; but perhaps not for much longer if Wal-Mart has its way.

THE GLOBALIZATION OF VERMONT

Clearly, in recent years, Vermont has experienced increasing difficulty in protecting itself from the debilitating effects of big business, big agriculture, big markets, and big government, who want all of us to be the same and to love bigness as much as they do. Over two hundred years ago, Ethan Allen and his Green Mountain Boys helped save Vermont from big New York landowners. Today the threat to Vermont comes not from the Yorkers but from globalization. The globalization of Vermont has progressed much faster and much further than anyone thought possible. The tiny, once idyllic, "locally owned and operated" Green Mountain state could become just another colony of a handful of transnational megacompanies.

Globalization refers to the integrated international system of mass production, mass marketing, mass distribution, mass consumption, huge financial institutions, and global telecommunications. This global network of markets, transnational companies, and information technologies effectively eliminates the need for national political boundaries, since money, capital, goods, services, and people flow freely across national borders. Political and economic power are transferred from nation-states to transnational megacompanies accountable only to their shareholders. Corporate rights always trump human rights. In many ways globalization is the final manifestation of cheap oil.

Since globalization is often achieved through coercion, intimidation, exploitation, collectivism, monopoly, and American military might, local cultures, local values, local communities, and local environmental concerns often receive short shrift. And Vermont is no exception to the rule.

Transnational megacompanies not only tell so-called "emerging market" countries (i.e., most of the world) what they will produce, how it will be produced, where it will be sold, and at what price, but they also influence local working conditions, wages, benefits, and labor laws. They dictate local governments' monetary, fiscal, trade, and banking policies. International money managers decide which foreign currencies are overvalued and which are not, as well as which countries should be punished for not playing by their arbitrary, self-serving rules.

Companies like General Electric and IBM have virtually a free hand to operate globally with little or no interference from government or labor. They play off one country or one state against the other in pursuit of low-wage, tax-free, regulation-free manufacturing environments. Vermont is simply too small to play effectively in this game; nor does it want to play.

The U.S. government and its Federal Reserve Bank, the International Monetary Fund, the World Bank, and the World Trade Organization are all committed to transforming the world economy into a giant global growth machine regulated by an international gambling casino in which resource allocation decisions are driven by a high-speed, multinational, high-tech crap shoot. Satellite communications, fiber optics, and the Internet make it possible to transform small, manageable local problems into unmanageable global problems overnight.

President Bill Clinton continually called for more trade, more budget cuts, more privatization, more foreign investment, more megamergers, more computer networks, less government control, lower interest rates, more IMF bailouts, and, as always, more economic growth. He wanted everything to be bigger, more complex, more high-tech, and more interdependent—bigger markets, bigger trade agreements, bigger loans, bigger bailouts, bigger banks and financial institutions, and bigger telecommunication networks. President George W. Bush's message is exactly the same.

Some economists justify globalization on the basis of the so-called "trickle down effect," in which the benefits of global trade to the superwealthy eventually trickle down to the poor. But World Bank figures suggest that the trickle down effect may not be working so well. In 1987, 1.2 billion people in the world were trying to survive on less than $1 a day. Now over 1.5 billion are trying to do so.

Although there are no more gold rushes, railroad bonanzas, cattle booms, oil and gas windfalls, or Western land grabs, the frontier spirit of the Wild West lives on in the hearts, minds, and behavior of Wall Street high rollers and many who inhabit the executive suites of corporate America. To assuage their narcissism, their greed, and their never-ending lust for money, power, and control, these high-tech desktop cowboys trade heavily on megamergers and acquisitions, lucrative stock options, government subsidies, and political favors to conquer one company after another.

During the eight-year Clinton administration there were nearly 75,000 mergers and acquisitions in the United States valued at over $7 trillion. This was considerably more than the twelve years of the previous Reagan and Bush administrations, known for their free-market oratory, in which there were fewer than 45,000 mergers valued at only $2 trillion. The trend is ever upwards.

This is not Vermont's style. It wants no part of this. But it seems to have little choice in the matter. To see how all of this has affected Vermont, consider the following. Most of the fourteen hydroelectric dams on the Connecticut River once owned by the Pacific Gas & Electric Company, based in California, were recently sold to a Canadian firm. The Vermont Yankee, the state's only nuclear power plant, is owned by Louisiana-based Entergy Nuclear. Two thirds of the hydropower generated in Vermont is exported, forcing the state to import thirty percent of the power it consumes from Hydro Quebec. Vermont and the rest of northern New England meet over seventy percent of their total energy needs from imported oil, making the region one of the most vulnerable to changes in the global economy.

When Vermont's largest, highest-paying, and most influential employer announced that it was laying off nearly 13 percent of its 8,000 employees, The *Burlington Free Press* headline read, "IBM Fires 988 in Vermont; Body Blow to Economy." Governor Howard Dean was quick to explain that IBM's decision was a response to a "global business problem" and had "nothing to do with the Vermont economy or even the American economy." But IBM does have an effect on the Vermont economy. For years it has threatened to relocate its Vermont-based computer chip manufacturing plant outside of the state, if state and local government officials did not meet its every demand for tax and regulatory relief. And just a week before announcing the aforementioned layoffs, IBM blocked passage of a legislative bill to encourage the use of renewable energy sources in Vermont.

The darling of so-called socially responsible investors, Vermont icon Ben & Jerry's, was sold a few years ago to Unilever, the Anglo-Dutch consumer goods conglomerate, for $326 million. It has already begun "downsizing."

Canadian-owned Banknorth and Husky are also important Vermont employers. The state's principal rail line, the New England Central, is owned by a Texas holding company. And *The Burlington Free Press* is controlled by Virginia-based Gannett, while a Colorado firm owns the Bennington and Brattleboro newspapers.

The automobile, interstate highways, shopping malls, fast-food restaurants, suburban sprawl, state government centralization, and the union (consolidated) high school movement have all taken their toll on Vermont towns and villages. Once-charming villages such as Essex Junction, Williston, Richmond, and Shelburne are little more than Burlington bedroom communities filled with apartments and condominiums. Strip malls in Burlington, Bennington, and Rutland are as unsightly as those anywhere. The state has been laced with fast-food restaurants— McDonald's, Wendy's, Burger King, Pizza Hut, and KFC.

And now there is the added threat from Wal-Mart. In a hard-hitting cover page article entitled "Is Wal-Mart Too Powerful?" Business Week said "Low prices are great. But Wal-Mart's dominance creates problems for suppliers, workers, communities, and even American culture." Many Vermonters agree. When the $350 billion Arkansas-based retail Goliath finally bullied its way into picturesque Bennington, it was a major defeat for thousands of Vermonters who had fought its entry into the Green Mountain state tooth and nail. Vermont was the last state to succumb to the heavy-handed retailer thought by some to be the Great Satan—the enemy of small towns and small merchants everywhere—and now the largest retailer in the world. Tiny Vermont was no match for the 6,000-store Wal-Mart empire with its seductive low prices, 150,000-square-foot stores, and 1.8 million employees. The interstate commerce clause of the U.S. Constitution makes it virtually impossible for a state to keep Wal-Mart out. Vermont now has four Wal-Mart stores, and seven more are planned.

In spite of the resistance, Wal-Mart is very successful in Vermont. It is successful because many Vermonters care more about "everyday low prices" than they do about the survival of nearby small merchants and small towns whose vitality depends, in part, on the viability of local businesses. In this sense, regrettably, Vermonters seem to be no different from any other Americans. The prevailing ideology seems to be, "I've got mine, Jack."

In addition to its low prices, Wal-Mart is known for its anti-union practices, race-to-the-bottom wages and fringe benefits, environmental insensitivity, the way it squeezes its suppliers, and its creation of urban sprawl. It has been accused of violating child-labor laws, ignoring state regulations requiring time for breaks and meals, coercing employees to work off-the-clock, employing illegal aliens, violating the Clean Water Act, and widespread sexual discrimination.

To put Wal-Mart's impact on tiny Vermont in perspective, consider the fact that between St. Johnsbury and Newport in the Northeast Kingdom of Vermont there are virtually no stores in dozens of villages. They have all been sucked up by the Wal-Mart across the Connecticut River in Littleton, New Hampshire. There is even a spur of Interstate 93 which extends into Vermont to make it more convenient for Vermonters to travel to Littleton.

The most blatant example of globalization and commercialization in the entire state of Vermont can be found in Williston, near Burlington, home of Vermont's two big box, megastore malls, Taft Corners and Maple Leaf Place. They are all there—Wal-Mart, Home Depot, Circuit City, Toys "R" Us, Pets Mart, Bed Bath & Beyond, Hannaford, Boise Cascade, Linen N Things, Staples, Dick's Sporting Goods, and Best Buy.

THE CHEAP OIL ENDGAME

Ironically, if one accepts the thesis of James Howard Kunstler's provocative book The Long Emergency, much of what was said in the previous section on the globalization of Vermont could become moot.

According to Kunstler the twentieth century in America was truly "the century of cheap oil." Cheap oil provided the material glue which held our nation together. It made World War I, World War II, and the Cold War possible, not to mention affluenza, technomania, megalomania, globalization, and imperialism.

But the American Empire may be on the verge of implosion, just like the former Soviet Union, though for quite different reasons, says Kunstler. The root cause of the demise of the United States will be the cheap oil endgame, otherwise known as "peak oil"—the point at which half of the oil that has ever existed in the world has been extracted. Unfortunately, according to Kunstler and others, "the half that was easiest to get, the half that was most economically obtained, the half that was the highest quality and cheapest to refine."

And how will we survive the cheap oil endgame? Only by becoming "increasingly and intensely local and smaller in scale." As the cost of petrochemical products soars we will have no other choice than to "downscale and re-scale virtually everything we do and how we do it, from the kind of communities we physically inhabit to the way we grow our food to the way we work and trade the products of our work," says Kunstler.

The end of cheap oil will precipitate the demise of globalization as well as the quality of life as we know it in the United States today. Large urban areas such as New York, Chicago, Houston, and Los Angeles may soon simply cease to exist as well as airlines, the interstate highway system, the automobile industry, corporate agriculture, and most multinational megacompanies. Large consolidated public schools and humongous state universities will go the way of the dinosaurs. And the Federal government will be impotent to protect us.

We will all be forced to simplify, downshift, and decentralize our lives and return to small towns, small businesses, small schools, and small communities.

Nothing better illustrates the likely impact of the cheap oil endgame than what is about to happen to Wal-Mart. To put it bluntly, Wal-Mart is about to get its comeuppance!

Wal-Mart's so-called "everyday low prices" for its imported plastic yuck depend heavily on foreign sweatshop wages, inexpensive shipping from abroad, a strong dollar, and cheap gasoline. The end of cheap oil will result in higher wages abroad, significant increases in shipping costs, the collapse of the dollar, and sky high gasoline prices dramatically reducing the amount of discretionary income available for consumers to spend at Wal-Marts. Wal-Mart's global empire will not only stop growing, but it will soon begin shrinking precipitously. The Wal-Mart phenomenon was but one example of the final blowout of cheap oil. Indeed, as Kunstler has pointed out, that's what globalization was all about.

With its small, clean, green, sustainable, socially responsible towns, farms, businesses, and schools, as well as its strong sense of community, tiny Vermont is uniquely situated not only to survive the cheap oil endgame, but to thrive.

IN SUPPORT OF THE EMPIRE

Whether Vermont is faced with the continuation of globalization, the cheap oil endgame, or a combination of the two, if it is to remain true to itself, it has no choice other than to maintain its commitment to a human scale lifestyle. To remain small, rural, radical, clean, green, democratic, and nonviolent, it must continue to resist being subsumed by an undemocratic, materialistic, militaristic, megalomanic, robotic, imperialistic, global empire of which it is a part. Does it really have any other viable option than to extricate itself from the United States of America? If that is the case, what is stopping Vermont from separating itself from the Union and going its own way as a small but mature independent republic? The answer lies in the politically correct, Vermont Democratic Party and its clone, the Progressive Party, neither of which has the guts to confront the fact that the American Empire has lost its moral authority and is going down.

Few Vermont voters seem to realize that every time they cast a vote for either Senator Patrick Leahy, Senator Bernie Sanders, or Congressman Peter Welch, they are lending their support to the largest, most powerful, most violent empire of all time—an empire which is thoroughly grounded in materialism, racism, and imperialism. By running for public office individual members of the Vermont Congressional delegation have implicitly cast their lot with the Empire. No matter how individual members may vote on particular issues, our Congressional delegation is an integral part of the problem, not the solution. Simply by agreeing to serve, individual members of the Vermont delegation legitimize a government that is corrupt to the core.

Although tens of thousands of Vermonters truly despise George W. Bush, most are prepared to do absolutely nothing about him or the Empire other than support some mindless, liberal Democrat for president in 2008, which is tantamount to doing nothing at all.

Vermont progressives all know in their heart of hearts that only the federal government can solve all of our problems. Unfortunately, the federal government is the problem! They fantasize about the Pollyanna-like myth of campaign finance reform, the liberal cure-all for everything. But that will surely never come to be, because corporate America likes things just the way they are.

Most Vermonters are too fat and happy to ever consider the possibility of actually confronting the Empire. So ingrained is the myth of Abraham Lincoln in the Vermont culture that our problems will have to become a lot worse before a majority of Vermonters will seriously consider secession as the ultimate form of rejection of a doomed nation. That day may be closer than most imagine.

As we said in Chapter 1, there is one and only one morally defensible position for Vermont regarding the American Empire—secession.

Chapter 3

THE UNTIED STATES OF AMERICA

That we will, at all times hereafter, consider ourselves as a free and independent state, capable of regulating our internal police, in all and every respect whatsoever—and that the people on said Grants have the sole and exclusive and inherent right of ruling and governing themselves in such a manner and form as to their own wisdom they shall think proper.

{ *Vermont Declaration of Independence,* 15 January 1777 }

On 28 October 2005, over 300 people in the Vermont State House in Montpelier heard keynote speaker James Howard Kunstler, author of *The Long Emergency,* warn that "the end of the cheap fossil fuel era" will lead to "the most serious challenge to our collective identity, economy, culture, and security since the Civil War." He further warned that "turbulence will be the rule," that "all bets will be off for politics, economics, and social cohesion," and that "the Federal Government will be impotent and ineffectual—just as it was after Hurricane Katrina."

He predicted that American life will become intensely and profoundly local, that we will have to grow a lot more of our food in the regions where we live, and that we are going to have to reconstruct local economies, local networks of interdependency. He also took note of the fact that Vermont is uniquely situated to meet the challenge of the cheap oil endgame because of its small towns, small businesses, small farms, and strong sense of community.

Kunstler spoke at the first statewide convention on secession in the United States since North Carolina voted to secede from the Union in 1861. The convention took place in the elegantly appointed Chamber of the House of Representatives. Permission to use the House Chamber free of charge required the approval of the Speaker of the House. Several Vermont legislators and a major gubernatorial candidate attended the convention. It was sponsored by the Second Vermont Republic—a peaceful, decentralist, voluntary association opposed to the tyranny of corporate America and the U.S. Government, and committed both to the return of Vermont to its status as an independent republic and more broadly to the dissolution of the Union.

Members of the Second Vermont Republic subscribe to the following set of principles:

Political Independence. Our primary objectives are political independence for Vermont and the peaceful dissolution of the Union.

Human Scale. We believe that life should be lived on a human scale. Small is still beautiful.

Sustainability. We celebrate and support Vermont's small, clean, green, sustainable, socially responsible towns, farms, businesses, schools, and churches. We encourage family-owned farms and businesses to produce innovative, premium-quality, healthy products. We also believe that energy independence is an essential goal towards which to strive.

Economic Solidarity. We encourage Vermonters to buy locally produced products from small local merchants rather than purchase from giant, out-of-state megastores. We support trade with nearby states and provinces.

Power Sharing. Vermont's strong democratic tradition is grounded in its town meetings. We favor devolution of political power from the state back to local communities, making the governing structure for towns, schools, hospitals, and social services much like that of Switzerland. Shared power also underlies our approach to international relations.

Equal Opportunity. We support equal access for all Vermont citizens to quality education, health care, housing, and employment.

Tension Reduction. Consistent with Vermont's long history of "live and let live" and nonviolence, we do not condone state-sponsored violence inflicted either by the military or law enforcement officials. We support a voluntary citizens' brigade to reduce tension and restore order in the event of civil unrest and to provide assistance when natural disasters occur. We are opposed to any form of military conscription. Tension reduction is the bedrock principle on which all international conflicts are to be resolved.

Mutuality. Both our citizens and our neighbors should be treated with mutual respect.

The objectives of the secession convention were twofold: first, to raise Vermonters' awareness of the feasibility of independence as a viable alternative to a nation which has lost its moral authority and is unsustainable; and second, to provide an example and a process for any other state that may be seriously considering separatism, secession, independence, and similar devolutionary strategies.

Two resolutions were approved by the convention delegates in the concluding session. One called for Vermont to return to its status as an independent republic—the same status it held between January 1777 and March 1791. The other called for the Second Vermont Republic to seek membership in the Unrepresented Nations and Peoples Organization.

Secession is a radical act of rebellion grounded in fear and anger but tempered by a positive vision of the future. It represents an act of faith that the new will be better than the old. Vermonters who advocate secession have found themselves going through a very personal and painful four-step process:

DENUNCIATION. Coming to the conclusion that the United States has lost its moral authority and is unsustainable, ungovernable, and unfixable.
DISENGAGEMENT. In response to that conclusion, feeling viscerally something like "I don't want to go down with the Titanic."
DEMYSTIFICATION. Coming to an understanding that, in spite of what we have all been led to believe, secession is a viable option constitutionally, politically, and economically.
DEFIANCE. Based on the first three steps, forming a resolve: "I personally want to help take back Vermont from big business, big markets, and big government, and I want to do so peacefully."

DENUNCIATION

The Manifesto statement, at the beginning of this book denounces the U.S. government in no uncertain terms, listing eight specific reasons why a state such as Vermont (or, for that matter, any state) might feel compelled to withdraw from the Union:

The United States is too big.
Our government is too powerful and too unresponsive.
It is controlled by corporate America.
We have a single-party political system.
Our government has lost its moral authority.
Our foreign policy is illegal.
We are at risk of terrorist attack only so long as we remain in the Union.
Our nation is unsustainable, ungovernable, and unfixable.

No further amplification of the reasons for seriously considering withdrawal from the United States seems necessary here.

DISENGAGEMENT

By far the most difficult step in the process of deciding to embrace secession is the emotional one of letting go of one's images of America as "the home of the free and the land of the brave" and "the greatest nation in the world." These images have been ingrained in most of us since early childhood. Reinforced by World War II, the Cold War, an uncritical education system, and our pro-American media, they are very difficult and painful to shake.

The decision to advocate secession involves reaching the point where you are unwilling to risk going down with the Titanic and must seek out other options while there are still other options on the table. Secession is only one such option. But, as we argued in chapter 1, it may very well be the only viable option available to us.

Can tiny Vermont help save the nation from further self-destruction by disengaging from it and by leading it down the path to disunity rather than mindlessly embracing the patriotic cliché "United we stand"?

Political disengagement may take many forms. It may take the form of protests against war, the military, racism, nuclear power, genetically altered food, globalization, the death penalty, poverty, and hunger. Alternatively, it may take the form of civil disobedience—deliberately violating laws which one considers unjust and risking arrest and even imprisonment. For example, tax protesters refuse to pay some or all of their federal income tax liability and thus risk arrest. In the event our government should decide to bring back the military draft, then draft resistance would once again become an important form of disengagement. But secession is by far the most radical act of rejection of the U.S. government.

DEMYSTIFICATION

Does a state have the right to secede from the United States? That depends, of course, to a great extent on whether or not one believes the United States is divisible. Millions of American school kids recite the pledge to the flag each day: "I pledge allegiance to the flag of the United States of America and to the republic for which it stands, one nation under God, indivisible, with liberty and justice for all."

While much attention has been paid in recent years to the phrase "under God" in this declaration, far too little has been paid to the word "indivisible." Just where does this idea of national in-divisibility come from? Is it based on the Constitution, or perhaps on the Declaration of Independence? Is it attributable to one of the Founding Fathers?

None of the above. Few Americans realize that the Pledge of Allegiance, popularized by the American Legion and other patriotic organizations, is the work of two obscure Boston writers who published it in 1892. It was not codified by Congress until 1942, during World War II. In fact, the Founding Fathers and the founding documents of the United States did not support the notion that the United States is indivisible; quite the contrary, the Declaration of Independence openly advocates secession (for what was the American Revolution if not an act of secession from the British Empire?), and the Constitution leaves the field wide open for secession.

For nearly 200 years, as Professor Donald Livingston has noted, Americans have disagreed over two contrary theories of what it was our Founders founded—the compact theory and the nationalist theory. The compact theory, first put forth by Thomas Jefferson and James Madison, holds that the Constitution is a compact of sovereign states, each of which has delegated enumerated powers to a central government as their agent. This theory was dominant in the early years of the United States; indeed, no nationalist theory appeared until the 1830s. As a result of widespread adherence to the compact theory, withdrawal from the Union was viewed until the Civil War as a lawful form of resistance available to any American state.

When Vermont voluntarily joined the Union in 1791 and became the fourteenth state, there is no evidence whatsoever to indicate that Vermont was committing itself in some irrevocable way. Indeed, the Vermont Constitution as it now stands makes it very clear that, if the government doesn't work, the people may change it.

That government is, or ought to be, instituted for the common benefit, protection, and security of the people, nation, or community, and not for the particular emolument or advantage of any single person, family, or set of persons, who are a part only of that community; and that the community hath an indubitable, unalienable, and indefeasible right, to reform or alter government in such manner as shall be, by that community, judged most conducive to the public weal.

Ironically, the region that most often considered disengagement from the United States before the Civil War era was New England. According to historian Thomas J. DiLorenzo, New England Federalists, who believed that the policies of the Jefferson and Madison administrations were "disproportionately harmful" to New England, thrice led independence movements aimed respectively at the 1803 Louisiana Purchase, the national embargo of 1807, and the War of 1812. Later, New England abolitionists also urged the northern states to disengage from the Union.

In sharp contrast to the compact theory is the nationalist theory championed in his later years by Abraham Lincoln, which holds that the states were *never* sovereign. According to this theory, after splitting with England the people of the various colonies were spontaneously transformed into the American polity. This body was sovereign and created a central government called the Continental Congress that authorized the formation of the states. The contract, once made between the people and the government, was irrevocable: a political marriage from which there was no divorce.

Lincoln really did a number on us a century and a half ago. Most Americans, whether they be black or white, liberal or conservative, believe that Abraham Lincoln was our greatest president because he freed the slaves. They also believe that he proved once and for all that secession should be avoided like the plague.

The knee-jerk reaction of most Americans to the word "secession" is based on the belief that not only did the Civil War prove that secession is bad, but also that secession is always associated with failure. Whenever secession comes to mind, one immediately thinks of slavery, racism, violence, and the preservation of the Southern way of life. Secession also flies in the face of a world which believes that bigger is always better whether it be big cities, big countries, big businesses, big schools, or big churches.

In his two books, *The Real Lincoln* and *Lincoln Unmasked*, Thomas DiLorenzo completely discredits Abraham Lincoln as a politician, a constitutional authority, and a statesman. He provides compelling evidence that Lincoln (1) did not save the Union, (2) did not want to free the slaves, (3) was not a champion of the Constitution, (4) was not a great statesman, and (5) did not utter many of his most important quotations.

Today neoconservatives are drawn to Lincoln because of his imperialism and his free wheeling interpretation of the Constitution. Liberals have mistakenly reinvented him as some sort of egalitarian populist, which he was not. Lincoln was a world-class political manipulator. So too is George W. Bush. Lincoln cleverly used the issue of slavery to turn the North against the South. Bush, on the other hand, has traded heavily on Americans' paranoid fear of terrorism to promote a global war with Islam and transform the United States into a technofascist state.

Early in his career even Lincoln himself supported the right of a state to disengage from the Union. On 12 January 1848 he made the following clear and passionate statement:

> *Any people anywhere being inclined and having the power have the right to rise up and shake off the existing government, and form a new one which suits them better. This is a most valuable, a most sacred right—a right which we hope and believe is to liberate the world. Nor is this right confined to cases in which the whole people of an existing government may choose to exercise it. Any portion of such people, that can, may revolutionize, and make their own of so much of the territory as they inhabit.*

Later, of course, Lincoln had a change of heart. To justify his invasion of the South and his scorched earth policy toward the eleven dissident states, he made preservation of the Union (and not, in fact, the abolition of slavery, as popular myth would have it) the moral imperative of the United States. In a letter to *New York Tribune* editor Horace Greeley in 1862, Lincoln said:

My paramount object in this struggle is to save the Union, and is not either to save or to destroy slavery. If I could save the Union without freeing any slave I would do it; and if I could save it by freeing some and leaving others alone I would also do that. What I do about slavery, and the colored race, I do because I believe it helps to save the Union.

Lincoln claimed that he had taken an oath to preserve the Union. But he had taken no such oath; rather he had sworn to preserve the Constitution, and the Constitution did not in 1861, and does not now, prohibit an American state from leaving the Union. When it became politically expedient to do so, Lincoln issued the Emancipation Proclamation. He also enshrined in the minds of all Americans the notion that what it means to be a good American is to ensure the survival of the Union at all cost—one nation indivisible.

Abraham Lincoln lived in an age of unabashed empire-building and of coercion of independent political societies into consolidated unions. What Bismarck was accomplishing in Germany with his policy of "blood and iron," what Garibaldi was trying to achieve in Italy, and what Lenin would later accomplish in Russia, Lincoln achieved in America through one of the bloodiest wars of the 19th century. Lincoln did not preserve an indivisible union from destruction, because he did not inherit one; rather, like Bismarck and Lenin, he tried to create one.

These days, thanks to the heritage of Abraham Lincoln, most Americans are firmly ensconced in the nationalist political camp, regardless of their political orientation. Liberals certainly have never tried to hide their affection for the nationalist approach. They believe that only the federal government can solve most of our economic, social, and environmental problems. They want government to be even larger. While some conservatives give lip service to the Jeffersonian, decentralist model of government, most are also strong political nationalists, and therefore they behave more like centralists.

For example, Ronald Reagan in his first Inaugural Address flatly rejected the nationalist theory: "The federal government did not create the states; the states created the federal government." But, while pretending to be a decentralist, Reagan may have contributed more to the massive concentration of power in Washington than any previous president with his multi-trillion-dollar peacetime military build-up. Reagan's nationalism always trumped his decentralist tendencies, as has also been the case with George W. Bush.

The Civil War, Abraham Lincoln, and the Cold War have all contributed to the view of most present-day Americans that secession is illegal, unconstitutional, unachievable politically, and completely unfeasible economically. In general, Vermonters' views on this topic differ little from those of the rest of the nation. There is only one problem.

They are dead wrong.

To allay these completely unfounded concerns about secession we shall consider three questions. Is it constitutionally possible for a state such as Vermont to secede from the Union? Would it be politically feasible? Could Vermont survive economically as an independent nation?

CONSTITUTIONALITY

In his book *A Constitutional History of Secession* (2002), John Remington Graham traces the history of secession and secession-like actions in America back to Britain's glorious revolution in 1689, when the Crown passed from James II to William and Mary without armed conflict but in defiance of the constitution of England. Certainly, the Declaration of Independence signed by thirteen English colonies on 4 July 1776 was an act of secession from England; but as Graham points out so too was the ratification of the U.S. Constitution in 1789 an act of secession from the original Articles of Confederation which went into effect in 1781. The fact that the Articles of Confederation contained a clause indicating that "the Union shall be perpetual" seemed to matter not. When Americans think of secession what usually comes to mind is not these earlier actions but the series of events leading up to the Civil War. Did the eleven states of the Confederacy have the right to secede? In an article entitled "The Foundations and Meaning of Secession" which appeared in the *Stetson Law Review* (1986), Pepperdine University Law Professor H. Newcomb Morse provides convincing evidence that the American states do indeed have the right to secede and that the Confederate states did so legally.

First, numerous states throughout both the South and the rest of the nation had nullified acts of the central government judged to be unconstitutional long before the people of South Carolina voted in convention to secede on 20 December 1860. Some of these acts of nullification took place in Kentucky (1799), Pennsylvania (1809), Georgia (1832), South Carolina (1832), Wisconsin (1854), Massachusetts (1855), and Vermont, which nullified the Fugitive Slave Act in 1858. According to Professor Morse, "Nullification occurs when the people of a state refuse to recognize the validity of an exercise of power by the national government which, in the state's view, transcends the limited and enumerated delegated powers of the national constitution." Those instances where national laws had been nullified by northern states gave credence to the view that the compact forming the Union had already been breached and that the Confederate states were morally and legally free to leave.

Second, and most importantly, the U.S. Constitution does not forbid withdrawal from the Union. According to the tenth amendment of the Constitution, "The powers not delegated to the United States by the Constitution, nor prohibited by it to the States, are reserved to the States respectively, or to the people." Stated alternatively, that which is not expressly prohibited by the Constitution is allowed. And nowhere in the Constitution is secession expressly prohibited.

The states delegated powers to the national government, not sovereignty. By international law sovereignty cannot be surrendered by implication, but only by an express act. Nowhere in the Constitution nor in the state ratification documents is there any express renunciation of sovereignty. Because sovereignty remains, all powers delegated can be recalled.

Third, while the Confederate states were in the process of taking leave of the Union, three amendments to the constitution were presented to the U.S. Congress placing conditions on the rights of states to leave. Then on 2 March 1861, after seven states had already left the Union, a Constitutional amendment was proposed that would have outlawed their departure entirely. Although none of these amendments were ever ratified, Professor Morse asked, "Why would Congress have even considered proposed Constitutional amendments forbidding or restricting the right to withdraw from the Union if any such right was already prohibited, limited or non-existent under the Constitution?"

Fourth, three of the original thirteen states—Virginia, New York, and Rhode Island—ratified the U.S. Constitution only conditionally. Each of these states explicitly retained exit rights. By the time South Carolina split in 1860, a total of 33 states had acceded to the Union. By accepting the right of Virginia, New York, and Rhode Island to withdraw, had they not tacitly accepted the right of a state to leave the Union?

Fifth, according to Professor Morse, after the Civil War the Union occupational armies were removed from Arkansas, North Carolina, Florida, South Carolina, Mississippi, and Virginia only after these former Confederate States were coerced into enacting new constitutions containing clauses prohibiting secession. But again, why would this have been deemed necessary if these states never had the right to secede in the first place? In addition, in the eyes of most legal scholars, agreements of this sort made under duress are voidable at the option of the aggrieved party; thus, there is absolutely nothing to prevent these six states from amending their constitutions again.

Sixth, Morse argues that the proper way for a state to leave the Union is through a state convention elected by the people of the state to decide one and only one issue, namely, the right of self-determination. According to Professor Morse, every Confederate state properly utilized the convention process, rather than a legislative means to withdraw, and thus followed the process that was understood to be correct.

Not surprisingly, there are many legal scholars who argue that unilateral secession is unconstitutional. They often support their argument through the use of the somewhat convoluted 1868 case *Texas v. White,* in which the U.S. Supreme Court ruled that even though Texas was once an independent republic it had no right to secede. "The Constitution," said the Court, "looks to an indestructible Union." About this Supreme Court decision that came right after the Civil War, John Remington Graham has written, "The opinion is pure sophistry and contradicts itself, resting on pleas that Texas was indestructible yet insane, sovereign yet incompetent to act."

Notwithstanding the *Texas v. White* decision, a substantial body of legal history—the tenth amendment; the history of nullification; the contingencies under which Virginia, New York, and Rhode Island acceded to the Union; the Constitutional amendments proposed while the Confederate States were withdrawing; and the conditions imposed on the six former Confederate States requiring them to incorporate clauses in their constitutions forbidding departure from the Union all support the proposition that it is indeed legal for a state to leave the Union. Furthermore, to deny the right of a state to secede from a larger government goes directly against both the language and the spirit of the founding document of our country, The Declaration of Independence, which goes on at great length in order to justify what is in effect an act of secession from the nation of Great Britain.

The Declaration begins by simply assuming that people may sometimes need to secede from their nation:

When in the Course of human events, it becomes necessary for one people to dissolve the political bands which have connected them with another, and to assume among the powers of the earth, the separate and equal station to which the Laws of Nature and of Nature's God entitle them, a decent respect to the opinions of mankind requires that they should declare the causes which impel them to the separation.

The Declaration then goes on to explain its theory of why and when secession is allowable, and even necessary:

We hold these truths to be self-evident, that all men are created equal, that they are endowed by their Creator with certain unalienable Rights, that among these are Life, Liberty and the pursuit of Happiness. —That to secure these rights, Governments are instituted among Men, deriving their just powers from the consent of the governed,—That whenever any Form of Government becomes destructive of these ends, it is the Right of the People to alter or to abolish it, and to institute new Government, laying its foundation on such principles and organizing its powers in such form, as to them shall seem most likely to effect their Safety and Happiness. Prudence, indeed, will dictate that Governments long established should not be changed for light and transient causes; and accordingly all experience hath shewn, that mankind are more disposed to suffer, while evils are sufferable, than to right themselves by abolishing the forms to which they are accustomed. But when a long train of abuses and usurpations, pursuing invariably the same Object evinces a design to reduce them under absolute Despotism, it is their right, it is their duty, to throw off such Government, and to provide new Guards for their future security.

The Declaration provides a long list of its grievances against the British government, in much the same way that parts of this manifesto list grievances against the current government of the United States—and ends with a statement that the colonies declare themselves free and independent; absolved from all allegiance and connection to their former government; and having the power to do all "Acts and Things which Independent States may of right do."

The crucial point is that it was not up to the British government to decide whether its actions were intolerable; rather, the colonists declared that it was up to them to make the decision for themselves. In the same way, it should be up to the people of Vermont to determine whether in their eyes the government of the United States has become intolerable.

POLITICAL FEASIBILITY

Ultimately, as was the case with the American revolution, whether or not a state is allowed to secede is neither a legal question nor a constitutional question, but rather a matter of political will. The ultimate test of sovereignty lies with the people themselves: How strong is the will of the people of the departing state to be free and independent of the control of the larger nation it was a part of? One of the questions raised most often in conversations about the idea of Vermont secession and the Second Vermont Republic is, "How would the United States respond to an attempt by Vermont to secede from the Union?" The implied question behind the question is, "Would the world's only superpower send troops to Vermont?"

Perhaps in contemplating these questions Vermonters can learn a lot from Eastern Europe's experience with Václav Havel's idea of the "power of the powerless." Within a matter of a few weeks in 1989 the iron-fisted communist regimes in Bulgaria, Czechoslovakia, East Germany, Hungary, and Poland were replaced by more democratic governments with little or no violence involved in the transition. Only Romania was a bloody exception to this rule.

The 1989 election of Solidarity leader Lech Walesa was the climax of a bitter eight-year struggle to bring down the repressive Polish communist government that involved repeated confrontation and engagement and eventually complex negotiations. During martial law, several hundred Solidarity leaders were imprisoned for relatively short periods of time. But, amazingly, only a handful of Poles were actually killed during this entire period. Czechoslovakian playwright Václav Havel's so-called velvet revolution also brought down communism in Czechoslovakia nonviolently.

Nonviolence is not a passive approach to conflict resolution, but rather a proactive approach that goes right to the crux of power relationships. It demands strength and courage, not an idle pacifism. It can undermine power and authority by withdrawing the approval, support, and cooperation of those who have been dealt an injustice. In addition, it elicits external support by drawing on the very real power of powerlessness.

Many American Sovietologists were surprised that the Soviet Union did not intervene militarily in Poland in the 1980s, as it had done in Budapest in 1956 and Prague in 1968. But Poland had a lot of influential friends and supporters, not the least of which were the United States and Western Europe. Certainly, the Soviets could have snuffed out Solidarity, but just as certainly that would not have played well in London, Paris, or Washington.

A secessionist Vermont could also find a lot of good friends— within the United States, in Canada, in Europe, and in the rest of the world. So it is certainly not a foregone conclusion that the United States government would intervene militarily in Vermont. Part of Vermont's strength lies in the absurdity of its confronting the most powerful nation in the world. Vermont's attempt to secede would undoubtedly attract sympathy from within the United States and abroad simply by virtue of its role as an underdog.

Conquering Vermont would be a lot like invading Liechtenstein or one of the more rural Swiss cantons. Besides the ridiculous power disparity, there is also Vermont's complete lack of strategic and military importance. The United States would not have much to lose by letting Vermont go.

In 1775 Ethan Allen took Fort Ticonderoga without firing a single shot. If Vermont can succeed in undermining the moral authority of the United States and convince the rest of the world that the United States government is corrupt to the core, then it too may be able to escape from the Union without ever firing a shot.

ECONOMIC FEASIBILITY

Making the Break

How Washington responds to a Vermont declaration of independence may depend in large part on how Vermont proposes to deal with four economic issues.

First, there is the question of compensation to the United States for government-owned property within the state including land, highways, buildings, and other physical facilities. The federal government might reasonably expect to be compensated for such property by Vermont.

Second, if Vermont decides to leave the Union, some people may prefer not to remain in Vermont. They may opt to move to Florida or some other state which remains in the Union and expect Vermont to pay for their relocation expenses.

Third, there is the question of Vermont's share of the national debt. For each $5 trillion in federal debt, Vermont's pro forma share would amount to over $10 billion. Currently the federal debt was is approximately $10 trillion. At first blush this number would appear to be quite intimidating—enough to make even the most ardent secessionist step back. If a state were obliged to pay its full share of the national debt as part of its secession price, then how could a state choose the secession option? By allowing the federal debt to grow without limits, have we not created the illusion that secession is completely unaffordable? Sadly, our national debt appears to be part of the glue that holds our nation together.

Fourth, as a crucial counterbalancing factor to the national debt share, a seceding state is not without major bargaining power, since it has a legitimate pro rata claim on all of the assets of the federal government—including land, forests, mineral reserves, waterways, highways, buildings, military bases, military hardware, gold reserves, foreign currency reserves, U.S. government loans, etc. Assuming that the combined assets of the United States have a value in excess of the national debt, which is quite likely, the claim that a state must cover its share of the national debt becomes moot, if giving up its share of assets is seen as an equal trade-off.

Indeed, for bargaining purposes a departing state might actually file a claim for a rebate from the federal government for its share of the positive net worth. The rebate, it could be argued, would cover the cost of the national debt and the costs of government property plus any relocation costs as well. Thus the settlement costs for a departing Vermont might actually be deemed to be zero. But that economic argument would certainly be a delicate one that would need to be made in a careful and rational way.

Long-Term

Could Vermont or any other state survive economically over the long haul as an independent republic? We believe the answer is decidedly yes: not only would Vermont survive, it would thrive.

For starters, Vermont's size does not in itself pose an economic problem. Few people realize that of the 200 or so countries in the world, nearly fifty of these have populations that are smaller than Vermont's 623,000. Some of them include Andorra, Aruba, The Bahamas, Belize, Brunei, Grenada, Kiribati, Malta, Qatar, St. Lucia, and Tonga.

Luxembourg, Liechtenstein, Bermuda, and Iceland, four of the ten richest countries in the world—each has a smaller population than Vermont and a higher per capita income. San Marino and Monaco are two other wealthy countries that are smaller than Vermont yet have comparable income levels.

Some claim that Vermont is so dependent on the federal government financially that it could never make it on its own. This simply is not true. For every dollar Vermonters pay to the U.S. government in taxes, they get back on average a dollar plus a few cents. This is hardly a big differential. Plus many federal projects come with all sorts of strings attached and with restrictions as to how the funds may actually be used, and they often oblige a state to commit its own funds to a project even thought it may be of little benefit to the state. The No Child Left Behind Act is an example of such a program.

A question raised frequently by Vermonters concerning the economic implications of secession is, "What about Social Security and Medicare?" If Social Security remains intact, then the U.S. government has a contractual obligation to pay recipients according to the prevailing payment schedule, no matter where they happen to live. That is, whether you live in England or the independent republic of Vermont, you are still entitled to receive the benefits which you have earned. Of course, the long-term future of Social Security under Team Bush remains somewhat unclear: there are some who believe that the aim of Team Bush is to extricate the U.S. government from Social Security altogether. If that does happen, the future of Social Security benefits for Vermonters becomes a moot point.

Since there are few benefits paid by Medicare for services rendered outside the United States, Medicare recipients might be among the short-term losers if Vermont were to secede from the United States unless Vermont could compensate Medicare recipients for these lost benefits. Indeed, Vermont, like Massachusetts has recently done, would need to invent its own health care system.

Even though most Vermonters are opposed to the war in Iraq and many of the Pentagon's policies, Vermont's pro rata share of the annual defense budget at present levels amounts to over a billion dollars. For those who oppose our policies of full spectrum dominance and imperial overstretch, this is a bitter pill to swallow.

Would an independent Vermont necessarily have to have its own standing army or defense capability? Costa Rica, for example, has survived since 1948 without any military force whatsoever. Of the four tiny, wealthy countries previously mentioned, only Luxembourg has a standing army of its own. And its army has only 900 active troops. Liechtenstein has been neutral since 1866 and has no standing army whatsoever. NATO provides for the military defense of Bermuda and Iceland. If Vermont felt a need for some form of military support to protect itself from attack by the United States it could always appeal to Canada, NATO, or the United Nations for protection.

Some skeptics of Vermont independence equate secession with economic isolationism and ask, "Where will Vermont get its food and its energy, if it secedes?" Presumably from the same sources that it currently does. Extensive trade with countries outside the United States is a very important aspect of the Vermont economy. Imports amount to around $3 billion annually and exports are a little less than that amount. Per capita exports in Vermont are the third highest in the nation behind Washington and Texas. Over 600 firms export nearly twenty-five percent of Vermont's gross state product, the value of goods and services produced in the state, which is the highest in the nation, and the rate of exports has been growing rapidly in recent year. There is no reason why this pattern should not continue after Vermont splits with the United States. While the U.S. government might try to impose a trade embargo on a seceded Vermont, it seems quite unlikely that Canada would abide by it, since Canada is Vermont's leading trading partner. Canada has never honored the American imposed embargo on Cuba.

While it is true that Vermont is not self-sufficient, few countries are. For example, the second largest economy in the world, Japan, has only limited supplies of strategic mineral resources and imports most of its food and all of its oil.

A free and independent Vermont could trade with whomever it pleased. It might belong to a trade and economic compact similar to the European Union involving other independent states. Vermont would not necessarily have to have its own currency. For example, tiny Liechtenstein uses the Swiss franc and Ecuador the U.S. dollar. Vermont could simply adopt the Canadian or U.S. dollar or possibly the currency of Quebec or New York, if either was independent and had its own currency.

A free and independent Vermont could also create its own business rules and regulations. If Vermonters grew weary of seeing Wal-Mart drive small, local merchants out of business, they could tell Wal-Mart to pack up and ship out. They could also limit the number of McDonald's and other fast food restaurants allowed to operate in the state. And to Virginia-based Gannett, Vermont could say that it is simply unacceptable for the state's largest newspaper to be owned by a megachain located in the suburbs of Washington, D.C.

With the recent spate of manufacturing layoffs in Vermont, some politicians are calling for lower taxes and fewer government regulations affecting business. But, unless Vermont were to reinvent itself as a severely underdeveloped country, within ten years IBM, GE, General Dynamics, and Bombardier will in any case have fled to Alabama or Mississippi, or to some other country such as Brazil, China, Indonesia, or Mexico. Once there are no more tax breaks or business concessions to be had in Vermont, the transnational megacompanies will vanish.

During the post 9/11 recession the Vermont economy fared much better than that of most other states. In part, this is the result of a strategy to make its institutions, environment, and culture more sustainable and less dependent on Washington, corporate America, and global markets. Such a strategy calls for the production of more high-quality, high-value products that can be sold at high prices to upscale, out-of-state customers whose demand is not influenced by the ebb and flow of the global economy. The strategy trades unabashedly on the Vermont mystique—Vermont's image as a state that is green and clean and produces premium-quality healthy products. For Vermont to survive economically after it achieves independence, it should just keep on doing what it's been doing so well—just being Vermont.

Physicians Computer Company in Winooski, which sells software to physicians worldwide employs such a strategy quite successfully. So too does Orwell dairy farmer Diane St. Clair, who ships 44 pounds of butter weekly to the nation's No. 1 restaurant, The French Laundry, located in the Napa Valley, for which she receives $10 a pound. And then there is the Strafford Organic creamery whose premium-quality ice cream costs more than Ben & Jerry's. Vermont's 260 certified organic farmers represent more of the same. Custom-made jazz guitars crafted by Brys Instruments under the hardware store in Shelburne sell for between $4,500 and $10,000.

Green Mountain Coffee Roasters is a profitable, human-scale, socially responsible business which walks the talk in terms of environmental integrity and pays its Third World coffee suppliers fair-trade prices to assure a continuous supply of organic coffees. The company's slogan is "The taste of a better world." Other premium-quality Vermont products with upscale prices include free-range turkeys, non-plastic tomatoes, drug-free beef, maple syrup, and a variety of specialty products. In recent years, an even-greater number of locally produced quality items have appeared. Many of these products are available at the Shelburne Supermarket and the City Market in Burlington.

The Vermont Department of Agriculture has found that the word "Vermont" on a product's label yields ten percent greater sales than would otherwise be the case. A product which has been given the so-called "Vermont Seal of Quality" will on average experience yet an additional ten percent sales increase. No one trades more heavily on the Vermont mystique than Ben & Jerry's.

Why couldn't Burlington, with its plethora of live music venues and recording studios, become the recorded music capital of New England, attracting regional artists as well as those from Quebec and the Atlantic provinces of Canada? Charles Eller's recording studio already attracts world-class artists to Vermont. The Northeast Kingdom could become even more of a haven for artists and writers than it already is.

The University of Vermont is well positioned with its new leadership to develop state-of-the-art programs in the management of small farms, small businesses, small towns, small schools, and small hospitals. It could team up with the Vermont Law School to capitalize on the

State's green image.

Many small Vermont companies have a high degree of environmental integrity, engage in participatory management practices, and maintain a high level of social consciousness. These are companies you would not mind having in your own backyard.

With the end of federal taxation in Vermont and the corresponding loss of federal services, of course state income, property, sales, and gasoline taxes will have to be adjusted. But if Montpelier's tiny state bureaucracy turns out to be more efficient than Washington's—and it is hard to see how it could fail to be more efficient, even after it grows to fill the needs formerly supplied by federal officials—then the net loss of federal revenue may prove to be a wash.

While those Vermonters who are currently employed by the U.S. government or are dependent on government grants and social welfare payments may incur some temporary inconvenience as Vermont makes the transition to an independent republic, these are short run problems which can easily be addressed by a small and responsive Montpelier based government located less than 150 miles from any place in the entire state. Montpelier is no Washington, D.C.

Ultimately, the cost of secession must also be weighed against the cost of doing nothing, remaining in the Union, and going down with the Titanic. Not a pretty sight!

DEFIANCE: A SECESSION PROCESS

Because secession has been viewed as a political impossibility by most Americans since the Civil War, no mechanism exists in our government to deal with this subject. Constitutional though it may be for a state to take leave of the Union, there are no guidelines to facilitate negotiations between separating states and the federal government with regard to government property, relocation costs, federal debt, and net worth. The unofficial policy of the U.S. government concerning secession is complete denial.

Thus in order to achieve its objective of breaking away from the United States, the Second Vermont Republic would need to invent its own rules for secession, giving attention to four different constituencies: (1) the people of Vermont, (2) the U.S government, (3) people in other American states, and (4) global public opinion.

With these constituencies in mind, the Second Vermont Republic conceives of the act of secession itself involving three very important steps:

* Approval by a statewide convention.
* Recognition by the U.S. government and other states.
* Diplomatic recognition abroad.

First, the Vermont Legislature must be persuaded to convene a statewide convention of democratically elected representatives to consider one and only one issue—secession. Such a convention might include 180 delegates, the combined membership of the Vermont House of Representatives and the Vermont Senate. Since the name of the game is statewide, national, and international credibility, at least a two-thirds majority vote would be required to move the process forward.

Second, once the articles of secession have been approved by the convention, the governor of Vermont would be empowered to deliver this document to the President, the Secretary of State, the Speaker of the House, the Chief Justice of the Supreme Court, and anyone else in a position of authority in the U.S. government who would be willing to receive them. What follows would be a period of constructive engagement by the Vermont governor with the U.S. government, modeled closely after the strategies successfully employed by Lech Walesa and Václav Havel in Poland and Czechoslovakia respectively, to free their countries from Soviet rule in the late 1980s. The aim of these negotiations is recognition of Vermont as an independent republic by the U.S. government.

Simultaneously, Vermont would need to seek diplomatic recognition from Ottawa, London, Paris, Berne, Stockholm, the United Nations, and other influential players on the international stage. As initial steps in this direction, the Second Vermont Republic has attracted substantial international media attention, particularly in Canada, Italy, Switzerland, Spain, and the rest of Europe.

The moment of truth will come for the Second Vermont Republic when the people of Vermont and the government of Vermont in Montpelier start behaving as though Vermont truly were an independent nation. At that point, federal taxes will no longer be paid, federal revenue flows into Vermont will cease, federal laws will be ignored, and the Vermont Legislature will begin the process of reinventing Vermont as an independent republic.

As for life and politics in the New Vermont, will it be business as usual? Or could Vermont become a libertarian state, like that proposed by the New Hampshire Free State Project, or maybe a democratic socialist state modeled after Sweden? Those would now, of course, be questions for the people of Vermont to decide.

THE GAME PLAN

Secession is a very tough sell, particularly in New England, where everyone knows that only redneck, racists from the South believe in secession. While most Vermonters are plenty angry at the federal government, few are actually feeling the pain associated with the demise of the

Empire. Supporters of the Second Vermont Republic do not possess the necessary elocution or literary skills to persuade Vermonters to secede from the Union. What will push them over the brink in favor of secession is the external environment.

Any one of the following events could dramatically shift public opinion in Vermont and elsewhere towards secession as a viable alternative to empire: Peak oil, economic meltdown, imperial overstretch, war with Iran, more environmental disasters, social upheaval, and international political blowback. Secession will gain real momentum when Vermonters and other Americans finally realize that the so-called war on terror is an insidious campaign to create fear and hatred among Americans and Europeans towards Muslims so as to rationalize a foreign policy of full spectrum dominance aimed at doing whatever is necessary to control their oil in the Middle East.

On 11 October 2003 around fifty people assembled in Glover, Vermont at the Bread & Puppet Theater in the Northeast Kingdom to organize the Second Vermont Republic. Early on the organizers of SVR ruled out the possibility of starting a new political party in Vermont. First, starting a new political party is a big legal and political hassle. Second, the track record of third parties in the United States is singularly unimpressive. Third, by far the two most successful political movements in the second half of the twentieth century in the United States were the Civil Rights and Anti-War movements. For these reasons we decided to organize as a citizens' network and think tank. In the eyes of the State of Vermont, SVR is a civic club. We also opted not to pursue tax-exempt status, since we are too overtly political. The group decided against any kind of formal hierarchical organization structure in favor of a completely informal modus operandi. Even today SVR is managed as a loose collection of independent projects in which no single person is in charge. The role of the center is to encourage and support new projects which support Vermont independence.

To educate Vermonters as to the benefits of secession and motivate them to actively promote Vermont independence we engage in the following activities:

❋ We commemorate three historical dates each year—Vermont Independence Day (January 15), Vermont Statehood Day (March 4), and Vermont Constitution Day (July 8).
❋ We publish an independent quarterly called Vermont Commons.
❋ We support two websites *www.vermontrepublic.org* and *www.vtcommons.org*.
❋ We promote town meeting resolutions in support of secession through the grassroots organization Free Vermont. (*www.freevermont.net*)
❋ We organize legislative briefings on Vermont indepen-

dence in the State House.

• We have a prestigious advisory board and an active speaker's bureau.

✳ With our sister organization the Middlebury Institute (*www.middleburyinstitute.org*) we promote secession nationwide through a national convention on secession and the publication of a registry of all secession organizations in North America.

✳ We hold statewide conventions as well as ad hoc meetings throughout Vermont.

✳ We seek membership in the Unrepresented Nations and Peoples Organization.

✳ With our partner Bread & Puppet Theater we engage in street theater, parades, and even mock funerals to commemorate the day in 1791 in which Vermont joined the Union as well as other events.

✳ We encourage secessionists to run for seats in the Vermont Legislature.

✳ We send out an e-newsletter to over 2,000 people monthly and occasional essays to several hundred people from time to time including the 180 members of the Vermont Legislature.

Throughout its short history SVR has attracted substantial national and international media attention including *Washington Post, Los Angeles Times, The New York Times, Christian Science Monitor, Adbusters, Utne Magazine, Ode Magazine, Orion Magazine, American Conservative, Boston Globe, Salon.com, The Nation, CounterPunch, Le Devoir* (Canada), *Montreal Gazette, El Mundo* (Spain), *Le Courrier* (Switzerland), Canadian Broadcasting Corporation, CNN, the BBC, and Fox News.

In addition to the 63,700 Vermonters who support secession, SVR has supporters in all fifty states as well as a dozen or so countries outside the United States including Australia, Canada, China, England, France, Germany, New Zealand, Sweden, and Switzerland.

There has always been a healthy tension between those who think SVR should be primarily a secessionist organization and those who think it should spell out exactly what Free Vermont might look like. *Vermont Commons* helps allay this tension by publishing articles which outline alternative political, economic, social, cultural, and environmental scenarios for Free Vermont. Ultimately, the people of Vermont will decide for themselves what kind of socio-economic, political system they want, not SVR.

Chapter 4

SECESSION AND INDEPENDENCE MOVEMENTS ACROSS THE COUNTRY AND AROUND THE WORLD

*A long habit of not thinking a thing wrong, gives it a superficial appearance
of being right, and raises at first a formidable outcry in defense of custom.
But the tumult soon subsides. Time makes more converts than reason.*

{ Thomas Paine, *Common Sense*, 1776 }

*Instead of union, let us have disunion now. Instead of fusing the small,
let us dismember the big. Instead of creating fewer and larger states, let us
create more and smaller ones.*

{ Leopold Kohr, *The Breakdown of Nations*, 1957 }

Although Vermont may be different from most states in a number of ways, most of the reasons why Vermonters are now talking about severing ties with the United States are no different from the reasons why those in any other state might want to secede from the Union. Whether or not you think your state should seriously consider secession as an option depends on your answers to the following eight questions:

＊ Do you find it difficult to protect yourself from big government, big business, and big markets?

＊ Do you think our government has become too centralized, too powerful, too intrusive, too materialistic, and too unresponsive?

＊ Do you believe our government has lost its moral authority?

＊ Do we have a single political party?

＊ Are you disillusioned with corporate greed, the war on terrorism, the Patriot Act, citizen surveillance, prisoner abuse and torture, homeland security, patriotic hype, the loss of civil liberties, environmental insensitivity, and the culture of deceit?

＊ Is American foreign policy immoral and illegal?

＊ Are you concerned about the risks of terrorist attack and military conscription?

＊ Has the United States become unsustainable, ungovernable, and, therefore, unfixable?

If you answered all eight of these questions affirmatively, then perhaps you should be helping to lead your state out of the Union. It matters not whether you live in a Red State or a Blue State, the logic of considering secession as an option seems clear and inescapable.

Today there are separatist movements in over two-dozen countries. Notwithstanding the strong European unification movement, during the last half-century separatist/independence movements have become much more important and widespread than unification schemes. For example, there are now nearly two hundred independent nations in the world, over four times the number that existed after World War II. The implosion of the Soviet Union and the breakup of Yugoslavia are two of the most important recent examples of this tendency, but there are many more that have already occurred and perhaps even more than that on the way.

We are witnessing the dismemberment and crumbling of multi-ethnic empires all over the world—the Soviet Union, Yugoslavia, India, Indonesia, and potentially China. The Soviet Union split into fifteen independent republics, many of which have their own independence movements. Czechoslovakia peacefully divided itself into the Czech and Slovak republics. Bosnia-Herzegovina, Croatia, Macedonia, Serbia-Montenegro, and Slovenia have all become independent nations as a result of the dissolution of Yugoslavia. Throughout Europe there are dozens of other independence movements in such places as Belgium, Bulgaria, Britain, Italy, Lapland, Poland, Romania, Scotland, and Spain. The Basque region of Spain is but one of eleven Spanish regions calling for more autonomy, and both Catalonia and Valencia also have full-fledged separatist movements. In Africa, hundreds of tribes are trying to shake off artificial boundaries imposed on them by nineteenth-century European colonialism.

After a near-miss in its 1995 referendum to achieve independence from Canada, the Quebec separatist movement remained in a state of limbo for nearly ten years until 2005. At that time a major corruption scandal involving the Liberal government precipitated a change of government in Ottawa and renewed interest in Quebec independence among French Canadians. Meanwhile, in 1998 the Canadian Supreme Court issued a ruling declaring secession to be constitutional and out-lining the necessary steps which must be taken by a province to secede from the Confederation. There are now also independence movements in Alberta and British Columbia.

In the United States some of the movements are regional, while others focus on individual states. For example, while many believe that Vermont would be an ideal state to test the limits as to how far the U.S. government might be prepared to go to preserve the Union, others have called for all of New England to become a separate Yankee nation.

Another regional movement is in the South. In the divisive 1860s the Confederate states tried unsuccessfully to lead our nation into disunion.

After military defeat, occupation, and Reconstruction, they were dragged kicking and screaming back into the Union. Some Southerners believe it's high time the South and the rest of the nation reconsidered dissolution. Founded in 1994, the League of the South is a secessionist organization with chapters in over half of the states in the United States.

Some Green activists in Washington and Oregon, two of the most livable states in America, have called for a merger of these two states with British Columbia to create the independent nation of Cascadia.

The United States already has separatist movements in over half of its states including Alaska, Hawaii, California, New Mexico, Texas, North Carolina, South Carolina, New York, Maine, New Hampshire, and Vermont.

California Governor Arnold Schwarzenegger recently noted that California has become "the modern equivalent of the ancient city-states of Athens and Sparta." With a population of over 36 million and a gross state product of $1.5 trillion, California has the eighth largest economy in the world. Governor Schwarzenegger added that, "We have the economic strength, we have the population and the technological force of a nation-state." Some Californians are calling for secession. Others would like to see the state divided into three separate regions which could evolve into independent states or nations.

Not surprisingly, many Texans would like to see the Lone Star State return to its 1845 status as an independent republic; just as many Vermonters dream of a Second Vermont Republic.

The two most influential state sovereignty movements in the United States are in our youngest states, Alaska and Hawaii.

The Alaskan Independence Party has nearly 20,000 members. Its challenge to Alaskan statehood is based on the claim that the 1958 statehood election was deliberately manipulated by the U.S. government, which wanted to assure an affirmative vote because of Alaska's strategic military importance in the Cold War.

Our conquest of Native Americans, Mexican Americans, Native Hawaiians, and Puerto Ricans was driven by the belief that our country had been chosen by God to rule the hemisphere, if not the entire world. "Manifest Destiny" enabled us to rationalize building a nation on Indian land with African slave labor, all in the name of progress. Not surprisingly, Native Americans, Mexican Americans, Native Hawaiians, and Puerto Ricans are all involved in independence movements today.

No ethnic group has a stronger claim for independence than Native Americans. In principle, there is no reason why there could not be several independent Indian nations. In practice, the existing Indian reservations are sparsely populated, poor, dependent on the government, and dispersed throughout the United States. There are only 2.5 million Indians left in the United States. Nevertheless, Indian nations might be sustainable in Arizona, California, and Oklahoma, each of which has more than 200,000 Indians living mostly on reservations.

As for Hawaii, in November 1993, President Clinton signed a law apologizing to the 140,000 native Hawaiians, who call themselves Kanaka Maoli, for the 1893 U.S. Marine invasion of Hawaii that deposed Queen Liliuokalani. That invasion led to Hawaii's annexation by the United States and eventually to statehood in 1959.

On 16 January 1994, the Kanaka Maoli proclaimed the independence of the Sovereign Nation State of Hawaii. In a 1996 state-sponsored plebiscite, 30,000 descendants of Hawaii's original Polynesians voted 3-to-1 in favor of creating some form of native Hawaiian government—paving the way for a constitutional convention to decide what kind of government they want.

Although Alaska and Hawaii are two of the best known separatist movements in the United States, they may be among the least likely to secede successfully because of their military importance to Washington. The White House is unlikely to let them leave until the right to secede has been clearly established, perhaps by a militarily unimportant state like Vermont.

As we have previously mentioned, thirteen percent of the eligible voters in Vermont are in favor of secession from the United States. To put this figure in historical perspective, it is important to realize that when the thirteen English Colonies successfully seceded from the British Empire, only twenty-five percent of the population actually supported secession. Furthermore, thirteen percent may represent the highest percentage favoring secession of any state in the Union. Take the Alaskan Independence Party, for example, founded by Joe Vogler in 1973. Although Vogler ran for governor in 1974, 1982, and 1986, he never got more than 5.8 percent of the vote. Few third party movements ever come close to achieving a thirteen percent support level.

THE MIDDLEBURY INSTITUTE

At a historical conference in Middlebury, Vermont, forty decentralists from eleven states and England met at the Middlebury Inn on 5-7 November 2004, just after the national election that gave George W. Bush his second term to discuss options and to plan for life after the collapse of the American Empire, which they agreed to be unsustainable, ungovernable, and unfixable. The conference, known as Radical Consultation II, was sponsored by the Second Vermont Republic and the British organization The Fourth World, which is committed to small nations, small communities, small farms, small shops, human scale, and the inalienable sovereignty of the human spirit.

At the close of the meeting, which was led by *Human Scale* author Kirkpatrick Sale and myself, over half of the participants signed *The Middlebury Declaration* calling for the creation of a national secessionist movement:

We the undersigned participants of Radical Consultation II held in Middlebury, Vermont on November 5-7, 2004, are convinced that the American Empire, now imposing its military might on 153 countries around the world, is as fragile as empires historically tend to be, and that it might well implode upon itself in the near future. Before that happens, no matter what shape the United States may take, we believe there is an opportunity now to push through new political ideas and projects that would offer true popular participation and genuine democracy. The time to prepare for that is now.

In our deliberations we have considered many kinds of strategies for a new politics and eventually decided upon the inauguration of a campaign to monitor, study, promote, and develop agencies of separatism. By separatism we mean all the forms by which small political bodies distance themselves from larger ones, as in decentralization, dissolution, disunion, division, devolution, or secession, creating small and independent states that rule themselves. Of course we favor such states that operate with participatory democracy and justice, which is only attainable as a small scale, but the primary principle is that states should enact their own separation and self-government as they see fit.

It is important to realize that the separatist and self-determination movement is actually the most important and most widespread political force in the world today and has been for the last half-century, during which time the United Nations, for example, has grown from 51 nations in 1945 to 193 nations in 2004. The break-up of the Soviet Union and the former Yugoslavia are recent manifestations of the separatist trend, and there are separatist movements in more than two dozen countries at this time, including such well-known ones as in Aceh, Basque country, Catalonia, Scotland, Wales, Lapland, Sardinia, Sicily, Sudan, Congo, Kashmir, Chechnya, Kurdistan, Quebec, British Columbia, Mexico, and the Indian nations of North America.

There is no reason that we cannot begin to examine the process of secession in the United States. There are already at least 28 separatist organizations in this country—the most active seem to be in Alaska, Cascadia, Texas, Hawaii, Vermont, Puerto Rico, and the South—and there seems to be a spreading sentiment that, because the national government has shown itself to be clumsy, unresponsive, and unaccountable, in so many ways, power should be concentrated at lower levels. Whether these levels should be the states or coherent regions within the states or something smaller still is a matter best left to the people active in devolution, but the principle of secession must be established as valid and legitimate.

*To this end, therefore, we the undersigned are pledged to cre-
ate a movement that will place secession on the national agenda,
encourage secessionist organizations, develop communication
among existing and future secessionist groups, and create a body
of scholarship to examine and promote the ideas and principles
of secessionism.*

A year later, Sale and Naylor launched The Middlebury Institute
with the intent of fostering a national movement to achieve the aims
of The Middlebury Declaration and to work towards the ultimate goal:
the peaceful dissolution of the American empire.

On 4 November 2006, the Middlebury Institute sponsored the first
North American Secessionist Convention in Burlington, Vermont. The
convention attracted delegates from 16 secessionist organizations in 18
states, including Alaska, Hawaii, Cascadia, Louisiana, South Carolina,
Tennessee, Virginia, Vermont, and New Hampshire.

What was particularly interesting about the convention was the
interaction between conservative, Red State evangelical Christians and
Blue State, secular liberals. Both sides sniffed each other out, pushed
each other around a bit on matters related to race, gay rights, and abortion, but no one crossed over the line defining civility. Everyone was
polite, but dead serious about why they were in Vermont. They had all
come to deal. Everyone agreed that what we all shared was a common
enemy—The Empire. There was also unanimous agreement on the
solution—peaceful dissolution of The Empire. The name of the game
was secession.

The convention issued a document outlining its basic points of agreement at the end of the meeting. *The Burlington Declaration* stated:

The Middlebury Institute publishes an online Registry of North
American Separatist Organizations *(www.middleburyinstitute.
org) which includes information on over thirty-five secession
groups in North America.*

ONE NATION DIVISIBLE

In the words of Kirkpatrick Sale, "the problem is not what the
nation-state *does,* but rather what it inevitably *is.* The solution, therefore,
lies in the eventual elimination of the nation-state for more democratic,
egalitarian, ecological and independent entities."If Vermont is successful
in extricating itself from the United States and reinventing itself as an
independent republic, then both Vermont and the remaining 49 states
might gain from the experience. Vermont's departure would send a clear
signal to Washington and the rest of the nation that enough is enough,
that overcentralization and an obsession with bigness don't pay. It could

set loose forces challenging the myth of Lincoln and the philosophical and political underpinnings of the Empire. Jeffersonian democracy might be given a new lease on life. The Empire might devolve into a confederation of relatively independent, loosely connected republics held together by a common monetary system—perhaps an economic union similar to the European Union along with a defense alliance similar to NATO.

States would be free to come and go. Some Canadian provinces and Mexican states might even be invited to join the Union. Real democracy might someday replace pseudo democracy. This is a vision worth fighting for.

Long live the Untied States of America!

Chapter 5

SOME MODELS FOR AN INDEPENDENT VERMONT

Switzerland solved the problems of minorities by means of creating minority states rather than minority rights.

{ Leopold Kohr, *The Breakdown of Nations,* 1957 }

I f the United States is not a sustainable nation-state, as many think to be the case, then how could or should an independent-minded state such as Vermont survive successfully as a separate republic? Should it be entirely independent, or should it attempt to create a federation with other small states? Are there any examples of smaller, sustainable nation-states or federations that might serve as a role model for a state like Vermont, should it decide to leave the Union?

There is at least one nation that might serve as a viable model for an independent Vermont, or perhaps for a confederation that would include Vermont along with several other smallish states (and/or what are now Canadian provinces): the Swiss Confederation.

With a population of only 7.3 million people, a little larger than that of an average American state, Switzerland is one of the wealthiest, most democratic, least violent, most market-oriented countries in the world, with the weakest central government and the most decentralized social welfare system. Founded in 1291 near Lake Lucerne, the Swiss Confederation may be the most sustainable nation-state of all-time.

Situated in the heart of Europe, Switzerland has always existed in a state of tension between opening and closing its borders to the outside world. Even today it has nearly one million so-called "guest workers." For centuries it has been an area of settlement and a transit region of European north-south commerce. The country's economy has long been geared to processing imported raw materials and re-exporting them as finished goods, such as specialty foods and pharmaceutical products.

The Swiss enjoy state-of-the-art technology, and their banks and financial institutions are among the most stable and financially secure anywhere in the world. The same is true of the Swiss franc.

Swiss Federalism. Over the past seven hundred years or so Switzerland has developed a unique social and political structure, with a strong emphasis on federalism and direct democracy, which brings together its 26 cantons (tiny states), with populations ranging from 14,900 to 1,187,600, and its four languages and cultures—German, French, Italian, and Romansch. The Swiss cantons enjoy considerably more autonomy than do American states. One finds a host of local and regional cultures and traditions melded into a patchwork of sights and events that are considered "typically Swiss." There appears to be less tension among competing cultures, religions, and cantons than one finds in the United States.

Switzerland has a coalition government with a rotating presidency, in which the president serves for only one year. Many Swiss do not know who of the seven Federal Councillors in the government is the president at any given time, since he or she is first among equals.

Direct Democracy. In Switzerland a petition signed by one hundred thousand voters can force a nationwide vote on a proposed constitutional change and the signatures of only fifty thousand voters can force a national referendum on any federal law passed by Parliament.

Several cantons still follow the centuries-old traditions of Landsgemeinde or open-air parliaments each spring. Others are experimenting with voting over the Internet.

However, it is at the commune level that Swiss democracy is most direct. Within the cantons, there are 2,902 communes in the Swiss Confederation, each run by a local authority. Just as the cantons enjoy a high degree of independence from the national government, within the cantons many of the communes also enjoy a high degree of independent authority and decision-making.

Swiss Neutrality. Switzerland has not been involved in a foreign war since 1515, and although it is heavily armed, it has remained neutral since 1815. It has never been part of a larger empire.

Swiss foreign policy is based on four premises: (1) Switzerland will never initiate a war. (2) It will never enter a war on the side of a warring party. (3) It will never side in any way with one warring party against another. (4) It will vigorously defend itself against outside attack.

According to the Swiss constitution, every Swiss male is obligated to do military service; women are also accepted into the military service on a voluntary basis but are not drafted. In case of an attack on the country several hundred thousand men and women can be mobilized within a few days.

Even though Geneva is home to many agencies of the United Nations, only recently did the Swiss vote to join the U.N. Although the Swiss do trade extensively with member nations of the European Union, the Swiss citizenry has consistently rejected membership in the EU, even though the Berne central government favors membership.

Neutrality does not mean non-involvement. In terms of foreign aid contributed to Third World countries, the Swiss contribute nearly three times as much, as a percentage of their Gross national income, as is contributed by The United States.

Infrastructure. Despite their fierce independence, Swiss towns, villages, and cantons do cooperate on major infrastructure projects involving the general public interest, including railroads, highways, tunnels, electric energy, water supply, and pollution abatement.

Many Swiss villages are linked by a network of passenger trains. Through efficient, high-quality railroads, village residents have easy access to neighboring villages as well as the larger cities such as Geneva and Zurich (both consistently ranked among the ten best cities in the world in which to live). The railroads provide a sense of connectedness to the rest of the country and to Europe as a whole.

Humane Health Care. In the highly decentralized Swiss health care system it is possible for patients, physicians, clinics, hospitals, and insurance providers to be in community with one another. Unlike in the United States, 95 percent of all Swiss citizens are insured against illness by one of four hundred private health insurance funds. The Swiss health care system is second to none, as is demonstrated by the fact that the Swiss infant mortality rate is among the lowest in the world in contrast to that of the United States which compares favorably with Eastern European countries like Hungary, Poland, and the Slovak Republic.

Quality Education. Although the Swiss constitution stipulates that "the right to sufficient and free primary education is guaranteed," there is no federal or national Department of Education. Rather, education is governed by the 26 different cantons. Swiss children are required by canton law to attend school. Kindergarten is voluntary and free. Some 99 percent of Swiss children attend kindergarten for at least one year, 63 percent for two. Instruction is given in the local national language, but each child also has the option to learn one of the other national languages. Those who plan to attend a university may go to one of three kinds of high schools specializing in either Geek and Latin, modern languages, or mathematics and science. Students who attend one of the seven public universities pay no tuition.

Decentralized Social Welfare. Swiss children are taught in small schools the virtues of self-sufficiency, hard work, cooperation, and loyalty to family and community. Since public assistance is funded locally, it pays off in visible ways for the community to discourage welfare dependency.

Aid plans are custom-designed with strict time limits. The objective is to help the client get back on his or her feet. For a few francs one can obtain any individual's tax return—no questions asked. This helps keep welfare clients honest. Thus the Swiss practice what conservatives preach but rarely practice—complete decentralization of the responsibility for social welfare.

Alpine Villages. Scattered throughout the Swiss Alps and neighboring Austria, Bavaria, and Northern Italy are dozens of small villages in most of these Alpine villages there is an inexorable commitment to the land A gift of land from one's parents carries with it a moral obligation of continued stewardship. Few would think of selling their land and leaving the village.

The church is often the center of village spiritual life, as well as social life. Friends meet at the market, the pub, the inn, the post office, and the churchyard to catch up on village news. The severe winters create an environment encouraging cooperation, sharing, and trust. The extraordinary beauty and the severity of the winters provide the glue which holds these communities together.

In these villages, in stark contrast to the rootless mobility that characterizes American life, one finds a sense of continuity where the generations are born, grow up, remain, and eventually die—a mentality which pervades all of Switzerland. Protective agricultural policies have made it financially viable for families to remain in the countryside. Conspicuously absent is the dilapidation, deterioration, and decay found throughout the American countryside—particularly in the rural South.

Swiss Agriculture. Even though only 4 percent of the Swiss people still live on farms, they manage to produce two-thirds of the foodstuff consumed annually by the entire country. So important is agriculture to Swiss culture, Swiss tourism, and ultimately the Swiss economy, that the Berne government has devised a creative system of direct payments to farmers over and above the income they receive from their produce. These payments remunerate the farmers for the services they are considered to provide to the population as a whole. These services include managing the rural landscape, managing the natural heritage, ensuring food supplies, and encouraging decentralization. Payments are made to farmers only if farm animals are kept under animal-friendly conditions, reasonable amounts of fertilizer are used, a suitable area is set aside for the maintenance of environmental balance, crops are rotated, soil quality is perfected, and plant protection products are used sparingly. The sophisticated payment formula also takes into consideration the farmer's age and income level, as well as the farm size and the number of farm animals. In Switzerland, sustainable agriculture is neither left to chance nor to the market alone.

Since small Swiss farms use fewer nitrates, pesticides, and herbicides, the Swiss wells and streams are much less likely to be contaminated than those in the United States. Swiss farmers have been pioneers in the field of environmental-friendly production methods, and serve as examples for other countries to follow. For example, recently Swiss voters passed a five-year ban on the use of genetically modified plants and animals in farming.

Environmentalism. Not surprisingly, there are not nearly as many federal government environmental regulations in Switzerland as there are in the United States. Concern for the environment originates at the village and canton level in Switzerland, not in Berne.

Although acid rain has taken its toll on Swiss forests, water pollution—with a few notable exceptions—is rare. However, Switzerland and France have recently experienced disastrous Alpine road tunnel fires. Environmentalists have opposed reopening these tunnels, arguing that heavy truck traffic pollutes the air and harms people and trees in areas of great beauty visited by many tourists. They insist that freight should be hauled in containers carried on trains rather than barreling through the Alps in convoys of polluting trucks.

Per capita energy use in Switzerland is only 46 percent of that in the United States in spite of the harsh winters experienced in the Swiss Alps.

Conclusion. Switzerland is not Utopia, and certainly the Swiss are not without their critics. Some view them as arrogant, narcissistic, racist, secretive, sexist, and xenophobic, —the latter despite the fact that they live together peacefully with many foreigners, currently nearly 20 percent of the Swiss resident population.

Swiss banks came under attack in the 1990s for the way they handled deposits of World War II Holocaust victims as well as Nazi gold deposits. Zurich has major problems with both drug abuse and AIDS. The bankruptcy of Swiss Air was also a major embarrassment to the Swiss, as was the air traffic control mishap over Swiss airspace which resulted in the midair collision of two jets.

The inescapable conclusion engendered by a visit to Switzerland is that Switzerland works. It works because it is a tiny, hard-working, democratic country with a strong sense of community. An independent Vermont, alone or in a federation with other states and/or provinces, could also work very well in much the same way.

New Acadia

Some proponents of Vermont independence would like to see it become and remain a stand-alone nation, completely independent of either the United States or Canada. Others have proposed that it join Canada or an independent Quebec. My own favorite fantasy would be for Vermont to join Maine, New Hampshire, and the four Atlantic provinces of Canada to create a new nation I would call New Acadia.

If Quebec were to split with Canada, the Atlantic provinces would be completely separated from the rest of Canada. But whether Quebec secedes or not, the Atlantic provinces will still be dominated by Toronto's size and financial clout, Alberta's oil, Vancouver's Pacific connection, and Ottawa's bureaucracy. So too are Maine, New Hampshire, and Vermont virtually powerless to challenge the will of California, New York and Texas. What big states and big cities want is what they get.

To put the matter in proper perspective, consider the following question: What do Maine, New Hampshire, and Vermont have in common with Boston, New York, Washington, Atlanta, Houston, and Los Angeles? The same thing New Brunswick, Newfoundland, Nova Scotia and Prince Edward Island have in common with Montreal, Toronto, Ottawa, and Vancouver. Virtually nothing! But what do these Northern New England states have in common with the Atlantic provinces? A lot!

Not only do both regions share a common Franco-Anglo (and Native American) heritage, but they are both sparsely populated. Their combined population is only 5.4 million—about the size of Denmark. There are no big cities in either region, only a handful of small ones like Halifax, Manchester, Portland, Saint John, and St. John's.

Although the mountains in New England are higher than those in the Atlantic provinces and although Vermont is only indirectly linked to the Atlantic, the two regions are amazingly similar geographically and equally beautiful. Their climate is quite similar, too—in fact on balance the four provinces have milder winters than their southern neighbors thanks to the warming effects of the Gulf Stream.

Nova Scotia, New Brunswick, and Prince Edward Island encompass the site of what was the first permanent French colony in North America, the region known as Acadia. According to some accounts, Acadia got its name from Italian explorer Giovanni de Verrazzano, who in the service of France explored the North Atlantic coast in 1524. Verrazzano called the area Arcadia after the idyllic region of ancient Greece known for the simple, quiet, contented lifestyle of its pastoral people. The r was later dropped.

Although two-thirds of the people living in the Atlantic provinces have some English ancestry, French influence remains strong, particularly in New Brunswick where 45 percent of the population have some French connection. The Acadian influence spilled over into both Maine and Vermont, where there are still some French speakers today.

Neither region treated native Americans very well. The Micmac still have some influence in the maritime provinces, as do the Penobscot and Passamaquoddy in Maine, and to a lesser extent the Abenakis in Vermont.

Life is lived at a slower pace and on a smaller scale in both the Atlantic provinces and northern New England. People are more laid back than they are in the rest of Canada and the United States, and small is still beautiful. For example, Vermont and Prince Edward Island share the distinction of having banned all roadside billboards. Freedom, independence, self-sufficiency, hard work, thrift, respect for individual rights, environmental integrity, and loyalty to family and community are among the common values shared by these regions.

Although trade flows between the regions are not impressive, their economies are quite similar. In varying degrees tourism, fishing, farming, food-processing, forest products, and mining are the most important industries in each area.

Few New Englanders have ever visited their bucolic neighbors to the North. Public transportation options connecting northern New England and Canada's Maritime provinces are minimal, and there are no good roads linking Maine and New Brunswick. Passenger train service between the two regions ceased to exist years ago (although those living in northern Vermont do have access to "The Ocean," a first-class over-night train between Montreal and Halifax on Via Rail and one of the best-kept secrets in North America). Unfortunately, attempts to connect the two regions with airline service have consistently failed.

On the more positive side, and perhaps a precursor of things to come, 300 business and government leaders from the Atlantic provinces and northern New England met in Saint John, New Brunswick in June 2006 to discuss ways to expand business and trade between the two regions. Discussions focused primarily on tourism, transportation, and energy.

My imagined new little country of New Acadia would be a threat to no one. It certainly would not possess the power to impose its will on meganations like China, Japan, or Russia. Why pretend otherwise? Power of that sort has certainly not proven necessary for such highly successful nations as Denmark, Finland, and Switzerland.

Isn't it high time for the people of these similar regions to tell the United States and Canada to bug off? Shouldn't we seriously consider forming New Acadia, combining our two regions into a new independent confederation? Our role model, Denmark, has the eighth highest per capita income in the world. Of the nine other richest nations in the world, two-thirds of them—Luxembourg, Liechtenstein, Bermuda, Norway, Iceland, and Ireland—are even smaller than Denmark.

Even if New Acadia's average income remained below that of Canada and the United States, the quality of life would be considerably higher The new nation would have less traffic congestion, less urban sprawl, less crime, less pollution, and less urban decay than most places in the world. In my vision it would certainly be a sustainable nation-state.

Our two regions are too small and unimportant to the United States and Canada for us to be able reasonably to expect either of these huge national governments to appreciate or celebrate our uniqueness. If we want to take control of our destiny in the twenty-first century, we must start now to develop a vision of what we could build.

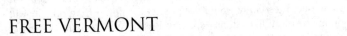

FREE VERMONT

If the scale of a country renders it unmanageable, there are two possible responses. One is a breakup of the nation; the other a radical decentralization of power.

{ Gar Alperovitz, *The New York Times*, 10 February 2007 }

When all is said and done, there is but one issue—the Empire. The American Empire is unsustainable. It has lost its moral authority. It has no soul!

Our government is corrupt to the core. It condones the needless occupation of Afghanistan and Iraq, a war on a brand of terrorism that we helped create, an impotent homeland security bureaucracy, corporate greed, coddling the rich and powerful, the suppression of civil liberties, environmental degradation, pseudo-religious drivel, prisoner abuse and torture, the illegal rendition of terrorist suspects, citizen surveillance, a foreign policy based on full-spectrum dominance and imperial overstretch, and a culture of deceit. This is the same government, according to Kirkpatrick Sale, that opposes "the Geneva Convention, the international criminal court, international law, the United Nations, test-ban treaties, the Kyoto Treaty, budget controls, civil rights, Social Security and an independent judiciary." As if that were not enough, Washington also promotes affluenza, technomania, e-mania, megalomania, robotism, globalization, and imperialism.

In the book of Ecclesiastes, we are reminded that, "there is a time for everything, a time to be born and a time to die." Will the sun soon set over the land of the free and the home of the brave, also now home to the most powerful and perhaps most destructive empire of all time? It is about time.

In fact, it is high time we take back Vermont right now from the insidious combination of big government, big military, big business, big markets, big agriculture, big computer networks, big financial institutions, big schools, big universities, big health care systems, and big religious institutions.

Unlike much of the rest of the Empire, Vermont still celebrates life rather than death. Its culture of the living derives its energy from the fact that it is small, rural, beautiful, democratic, nonviolent, noncommercial, egalitarian, humane, independent, and very radical. In Vermont the politics of human scale always trumps the politics of the left and the politics of the right.

As for America as a whole, it's time for it to decentralize, downsize, and eventually dissolve. Vermont can lead the way. Both America and the rest of the world need an independent Vermont as a reminder that life can still be lived on a human scale. Small is beautiful. Secession is truly our only morally defensible alternative.

So, as our neighbors and allies in Quebec say, *Vive Le Vermont Libre!* The time for action is now.

THE SECOND
VERMONT REPUBLIC NETWORK

Second Vermont Republic
{ Think Tank and Citizens' Network }
www.vermontrepublic.org
TELEPHONE
802-425-4133
ADDRESS
P.O. Box 544
Charlotte, VT 05445

Vermont Commons
{ Award-winning Journal }
www.vtcommons.org
E-MAIL
editor@vtcommons.org
ADDRESS
308 Wallis Drive
Waitsfield, VT 05673

Free Vermont
{ Grass Roots and Town Meetings }
www.freevermont.net
E-MAIL
volunteer@freevermont.net

Middlebury Institute
{ National and International Outreach }
www.MiddleburyInstitute.org
E-MAIL
Director@MiddleburyInstitute.org
ADDRESS
127 E. Mountain Road S.
Cold Spring, NY 10516

ACKNOWLEDGEMENTS

Although the Second Vermont Republic did not come into existence until 11 October 2003, work on this book began over a year earlier. Literally hundreds of members of the Vermont independence movement have helped shape the Second Vermont Republic and the ideas contained herein. However, five SVR members deserve special mention—Frank Bryan, Ian Baldwin, Donald Livingston, Kirkpatrick Sale, and Rob Williams.

University of Vermont Political Science Professor Frank Bryan, the elder statesman of Vermont independence, has been writing and talking about the possibility of Vermont seceding from the Union since the late 80s. After Alexander Solzhenitsyn left Vermont and returned to Russia, Bryan became the single most interesting person living here. The book benefited immeasurably from frequent meetings with him at Papa Nick's restaurant in Hinesburg.

In April 2005 publisher Ian Baldwin and editor Rob Williams launched the award-winning quarterly *Vermont Commons*, devoted to Vermont independence. They were both major players in defining and influencing the conversations about a free Vermont.

From day one, Emory University Philosophy Professor Donald W. Livingston has been the philosophical guru of the Second Vermont Republic. *Human Scale* author Kirkpatrick Sale has been an important consultant to the Vermont independence project. His Middlebury Institute is committed to placing secession on the national radar screen.

Duke University Press Editorial Director Stephen A. Cohn devoted countless hours to editing, rewriting, and polishing this manuscript. Words alone cannot express my appreciation for the major contributions which he made to this book.

Kimberly Malone skillfully edited and typed endless drafts—always with good cheer.

And last, but by no means least, my wife Magdalena and son Xander had to listen to me talk about Vermont independence for over five years at the dinner table. They not only listened, but raised important questions and made helpful suggestions.

And, of course, the usual caveat applies…

ABOUT THE AUTHOR

Professor Emeritus of Economics at Duke University, Thomas H. Naylor is a writer and a political activist who has taught at Middlebury College and the University of Vermont. For thirty years, he taught economics, management science, and computer science at Duke.

As an international management consultant specializing in strategic management, Dr. Naylor has advised major corporations and governments in over thirty countries. During the 1970s he was President of a 50-person computer software firm whose clients were Fortune 500 companies worldwide.

Professor Naylor was one of the first to predict in *The New York Times* the unexpected changes in the Soviet Union and Eastern Europe, where he traveled frequently in the 1980s. From this experience he has concluded the American Empire, not unlike its former nemesis the USSR, has lost its moral authority and is no longer sustainable. This led him to help launch the Second Vermont Republic, Vermont's independence movement, in 2003. *Utne Magazine* editor Jay Walljasper dubbed him "Tom Paine for the 21st century."

The New York Times, International Herald Tribune, Los Angeles Times, Adbusters, Christian Science Monitor, The Nation, and *Business Week* have published his articles. He has appeared on ABC's *Nightline*, CBS News, CBC's *The National*, CNN, C-SPAN2, National Public Radio, and Minnesota Public Radio. The most recent of his thirty books are *Downsizing the U.S.A., Affluenza,* and *The Vermont Manifesto*. He is currently completing a book entitled *Rebél*. For additional information, visit *www.vermontrepublic.org*.

www.FeralHouse.com

✻

www.vermontrepublic.org